CW00404621

SHAOLIN TEMPLE
KUNG FU

SHAOLIN TEMPLE KUNG FU

DAVID MITCHELL

STANLEY PAUL

LONDON · SYDNEY · AUCKLAND · JOHANNESBURG

Stanley Paul and Co Ltd
An imprint of the Random Century Group
20 Vauxhall Bridge Road, London SW1V 2SA

Random Century Australia (Pty) Ltd
20 Alfred Street, Milsons Point, Sydney NSW 2061

Random Century New Zealand Ltd
191 Archers Road, PO Box 40–086, Glenfield, Auckland 10, New Zealand

Random Century South Africa Ltd
PO Box 337, Bergvlei 2012, South Africa

First published 1990

Photoset in Plantin by Speedset Ltd, Ellesmere Port
Printed and bound in Great Britain by
Scotprint Ltd, Musselburgh, Scotland

British Library Cataloguing in Publication Data
Mitchell, David
Shaolin Temple Kung Fu : an official Martial Arts
Commission book.
1. Kung Fu
I. Title   II. Martial Arts Commission
796.8′159

ISBN 0–09–174012–6

Contents

Acknowledgements

I gratefully acknowledge the assistance of Alan Campbell and Colin Jones in the production of this book. I would also like to thank Robert Clark for the use of his excellent training facilities.

The author and publishers would like to thank Sylvio Dokov for the photography.

Introduction

If one were to accept the legends concerning Shaolin Temple at their face value, then this would entail accepting that all the very best of martial art in the vast nation of China originated in one small place and over a period of less than ten years. More than this, one would have to accept that what is now a diverse fighting system originated from a single Indian Buddhist monk! Though this might seem incredible, it is nevertheless held to be the case by a large number of modern day martial arts practitioners.

We should, it seems, accept that when Bodhidharma introduced *Ch'an* (Zen) Buddhism to the temple, he became concerned at the monks' inability to remain in seated meditation for long periods and so taught them a series of exercises. Interestingly, one account claims that Bodhidharma himself sat in meditation for nine years, during which time his legs withered away from lack of use! Ignoring that aside for the present, the story continues by claiming that these exercises – none of which, so far as we can see, involved any kind of weapons-usage – formed the foundation of subsequent practice. We will examine what are now thought to be these exercises a little later, and the reader is invited to ponder how a comprehensive armed/unarmed fighting system could have originated from what seem to be no more than yoga-type breathing exercises. Also, we know that Bodhidharma travelled to other monasteries where, presumably, the monks were just as 'unfit' as they were at Shaolin. Why then, if Bodhidharma is the sole source of martial knowledge, did he not plant the seeds of martial art development in these other places too? He appears not to have done so, and the next question might be, why not? Perhaps he taught no martial art exercises at Shaolin, much less anywhere else.

But, if the legend is nevertheless to be believed, the legacy of Bodhidharma led to the development of a fighting system which made use of the military weapons of the day plus unarmed combat

Legend has it that Bodhidharma taught martial arts to the monks at Shaolin to make them better able to withstand the rigours of seated meditation

of such sophistication that it formed the basis for many subsequent lines of development down to the present time. Twice we learn of a mere handful of monks going against a large corps of soldiers and soundly defeating them. Then the monastery is razed to the ground by an emperor afraid of their military prowess (this at least shows the monks weren't invincible!) and only five survivors are left to pass on the temple's martial art heritage.

10

*The six-foot staff is regarded by many as the symbol of Shaolin
martial art excellence*

We will critically examine these claims and try to arrive at a
more reasonable picture of what may have actually transpired.
This is worth doing because we know that Shaolin existed – indeed
it exists today, though admittedly in a many times over rebuilt
form. Furthermore, there are too many diverse legends attesting
to the martial skill of Shaolin monks for it to have all been
fabrication. But is it still possible to peel back the many layers of

11

later accounts and get a brief glimpse of the original skills? The lack of historical data means that ultimately any representation is open to criticism but I believe the picture painted by these pages is the most accurate to date.

I believe we can arrive at a credible assessment of Bodhidharma's input to martial art practice. Furthermore, I believe we can suggest good reasons why martial art practice arose amongst the Buddhist community of Shaolin independently of their apparent lack of fitness. We can review the weapons available to the monks and see how these might have been used. In particular, we may be able to understand how and why the six-foot staff came to be seen as a symbol of Shaolin martial arts prowess. Indeed, the armed systems of combat are a study in themselves! During this examination, I believe we can show how the syncretism which existed between Taoism and early Buddhism may have introduced some of the so-called 'internal systems'. Previously we have thought of these as entirely different from the essentially 'external' nature of Shaolin martial art, and their apparent presence at Shaolin has caused some martial arts historians to stumble.

We know a little about the philosophy taken up by the warrior-monks of Shaolin. Though in principle pacifist, it does have a life-denying core that makes 'struggling insanely in the very jaws of death' as insignificant a matter as taking tea! Even a small number of warriors holding such a philosophy would prove difficult to deal with! The mental and the physical aspects of the Shaolin system go hand in hand, and to separate them makes a nonsense of Shaolin martial art.

Finally, wherever possible I have avoided the usage of Chinese expressions in this text and have relied instead upon what I believe is a practical (if not entirely accurate) and comprehensible translation.

David Mitchell
Lancaster University
June 1990

1 The Development and History of Shaolin Temple

The Introduction of Buddhism to China

Shaolin is a Buddhist temple, so it is appropriate to begin our examination by looking at the historical circumstances relating to the introduction of Buddhism to China, and its subsequent adoption by that nation.

Buddhism was introduced into China from India, sometime during the Han Dynasty (202 BC–AD 220) and rapidly spread thoughout the country. The reasons why this should be so are not entirely clear, though it has been suggested that the philosophical content of Buddhism struck a harmonious chord in the Chinese mentality of that period. Whereas the climate of India generally meant that solitary monks could live a life exposed to the elements, that of China called for proper shelter. Thus, permanent communities of the faithful arose.

The collapse of the Han Dynasty was accompanied by serious social upheavals during which the Buddhist notions of self-salvation may have seemed a way of coping. Thus it was that Buddhism continued to flourish during the Northern and Southern Dynasty period (AD 420–589), and received much royal support. In AD 476, Emperor Xiao Wen of the Northern Wei Dynasty ordered more than 100 men and women into the Buddhist priesthood. And not content with so directing them, he personally cut their hair and issued them with their robes! By March 477, the number of temples in the capital had increased to 100, with approximately 2,000 monks and nuns in attendance. There were a further 6,478 Buddhist temples outside of the capital, with 77,258 monks and nuns.

Foreign Buddhists were welcomed, especially those from India where Buddhism had originated. One of these was the Indian monk Budhabhadra (*Ba Tuo* in Chinese). Budhabhadra lived from AD 359–429 and is known for the contribution he made to Chinese Buddhism through his translation into Chinese of all 60 books of the Avatamsaka sutra. Budhabhadra had studied *Hinayanist* teachings but he was sometimes wrongly thought to have taught *Mahayana* ('Great Vehicle') doctrines. The latter were more popular with the Chinese because their notions of perfect wisdom were in accord with the Chinese spirit of that age.

Some historical sources claim that Budhabhadra met Emperor Xiao Wen in or around AD 496 (i.e., 67 years after the former's death!) and accompanied him to Lo-yang. Budhabhadra was said to have been fond of solitary meditation amongst the woods and peaks of nearby Sung Shan and, seeing this, the emperor decided to build Shaolin there. However, as we have noticed, this version does not take into account Budhabhadra's earlier death and it is likely that he has been confused with Bodhidharma. Nevertheless, as we already know, Bodhidharma visited an already existing monastery at Shaolin! This has been included to show just how unreliable some early sources can be.

Bodhidharma

Buddhism was well received by the native Tao religion and, at first, both Hinayana and Mahayana doctrines were practised side by side – sometimes in the same monastery. It is into this setting that Bodhidharma appears. Bodhidharma was said to have come from southern India. His social status appears to have been that of the Brahman caste, and other legends claim that he was of royal blood. If any claim to his having taught martial art methods is to be entertained, then a noble connection might explain it.

Bodhidharma is regarded as the first Chinese patriarch of Ch'an Buddhism, though claims that he founded the sect in China are contested. Even if he is not the sole founder, his name is widely used in connection with the subsequent transmission of Ch'an down through the generations. It is also claimed that he was the twenty-eighth Indian patriarch, with an authority going back to Buddha via the latter's disciple, Kasyapa. The details of Bodhidharma's birth and death are unknown, though legends abound. However, all the diverse accounts seem inclined to describe him as living to a ripe old age, despite a number of attempts at poisoning him! Indeed, sketches always show him as a toothless old man with staring eyes, so it is at least possible that claims that he lived to be over 100 may not be too far from the truth.

Some sources claim that Bodhidharma entered north-western

Bodhidharma is regarded as the originator of martial development at Shaolin, though there is virtually no hard evidence to support this view

China after an arduous journey. Others report that he entered via south-western China. However, attempts to expand the geographical area of his travels may stem from a desire to emphasize his importance by exaggerating the scope of his ministry. He is alleged to have had an audience with Emperor Wu (AD 502–50), the founder of the Liang Dynasty, and in the course of this audience he pointed out the futility of building Buddhist temples and reciting sutras. Following this audience, he is said to have crossed the Yangtze River by unorthodox means and travelled to Shaolin, where he sat in meditation for nine years. He attracted a number of disciples, of whom Tao-yu and Hui-ko are the first two mentioned.

Legend further has it that he travelled on from Shaolin to avoid being secularized during the subsequent attack on Buddhism by

Emperor Wu Ti, and continued to teach Ch'an Buddhism in southern China until he eventually died on the banks of the Luohe River. The works of Bodhidharma were compiled, it is said, by another of his disciples, T'an-lin, but unfortunately they make no reference to any martial art practice or exercises. Ch'an tradition claims that Bodhidharma wrote six treatises in total.

The Geography, Origins and Structure of Shaolin Temple

Shaolin Temple is situated in the Lo-yang – Cheng-chou – K'ai-feng Region of Honan Province. It is approximately 625 kilometres south-south-west of Peking and 820 kilometres west by north of Shanghai. Honan is one of the smallest Chinese provinces, but it is one of the most densely populated. It is also one of the oldest settled areas in China and its northern reaches were the homeland of the Shang bronze culture. The area of Lo-yang became the second capital – after the first capital was changed – of the Chou Dynasty, and the capital of the Han Dynasty. In the 10th century, K'ai-feng became the capital of the Sung dynasty. At that time it was one of the richest commercial cities in China. Cheng-chou is the seat of one of the ancient Shang capitals.

The Lo-yang – Cheng-chou – K'ai-feng region occupies part of the middle Huang Ho Valley, an important and ancient east-west route. The Honan mountains which take up a third of the province are the eastern extremity of the great Chin-ling range and in the hills south of the Lo valley is the ancient holy mountain of Sung Shan (1,359 metres). This region is rather sparsely populated by comparison with the rest of the province and much of it still has forest cover.

The monastery is situated on a south-facing aspect, amongst gullies and cliffs at the foot of Wu Ru Feng ('Five-breast Peak'). It is 13 kilometres north-west of the county seat of T'eng Feng and faces the cliffs of Shaoshi Mountain. As the temple is situated deep in the woodland (*Lin* in Chinese) of Shaoshi Mountain, it is called 'Shaolin'. The Shaoxi Stream flows in front of the temple entrance and it is still possible to find relics of ancient cultures there. Because the temple is at a high elevation, it is cool in summer and positively cold in winter!

Sung Shan has been the home of many temples – some say as many as 100 – but the most important of these is Shaolin. The exact date of its first building is unknown, though it is confidently placed sometime within the Northern Wei Dynasty (AD 386–534).

AD 496 seems to be the preferred time of its construction. The commissioning ruler is also unknown. Some authorities claim that it was the very first Ch'an Buddhist temple built in China. Since its original construction, the temple has been added to (as well as being burnt down and successively rebuilt) throughout the 1,400 years or so of its existence so that it now covers a large area.

The Forest of Pagodas is located 250 metres west of the monastery and Bodhidharma Pavilion is on the hill to the north-west. Chang Zhu Yuan is regarded as the temple proper. It was constructed during the T'ang Dynasty and contains a number of courtyards in which the monks practised martial art.

One of the two archways near the entrance to the temple bears the inscription 'Founded by Ba Tuo'. Another inscription affirms that the monastery is the seat of Mahayana Buddhism. These archways, however, are very much later and are reckoned to date from 1543–55, during the reign of Emperor Jia Jing of the Ming Dynasty.

Much historical information has been obtained from studying inscriptions written onto stone stelae. Some inscriptions go all the way back to the T'ang period and are still perfectly legible. Particularly relevant are ones such as 'Watching wu shu in Shaolin' by Cheng Shao. This is dated 1625 and indicates that martial arts practice at the monastery was thriving then.

Daxiong ('Mahavira') Hall contained part of the temple's arsenal of weapons. It was referred to as 'The Great Hall' and was one of the three destroyed by a fire in 1928. Weapons were also stored in the ruined Dharma Hall, alongside Buddhist scriptures, but this was a much later construction.

Near the ruined bell tower is a brick building housing two tablets. One is of particular importance for martial arts historians; this is the 'Tablet For Li Shi-min', dictated in AD 621 and erected in 728. Li Shi-min was later to become the second T'ang emperor Tai T'sung. The tablet is signed by Li himself and attests to the fact that he received aid from the monks of Shaolin during his battle with the would-be usurper, Wang Shi-chung.

The Thousand Buddha Hall was built in 1588 during the Ming Dynasty, using materials taken from earlier buildings. It has been twice repaired since that time (in 1639 and in 1775) and is interesting to martial artists in that it appears to have been a training area. There are 48 depressions which look as though they were worn away by generations of martial artists using the same movements in the same area.

The White Garment Hall is also of great interest in that it contains the famous wall murals which show martial arts practice at the Temple. The north wall mural depicts 16 groups of monks practising unarmed combat. One of these shows the legendary boxer Zhan Ju sparring with three other monks, one of whom has already been felled. The south wall shows 15 groups of monks practising with staffs, swords, spears, knives, halberds and peculiar circular hooks. The back wall depicts 13 monks aiding Li Shi-min and this is interesting because other historical sources claim that 14 monks were involved. Another part of the wall shows a member of the Shaolin staff frightening away a group of rebellious peasants.

Bodhidharma Pavilion is bordered by gullies on three sides and is backed by Wu Ru Feng. A stone tablet, erected in 1605, commemorates the place where Bodhidharma sat and meditated for nine years. A path ascends Wu Ru Feng from near the Bodhidharma Pavilion and leads to a cave in which Bodhidharma is believed to have meditated. The cave is dug into the side of a cliff face and is over six metres deep. It contains what is called 'The Shadow Rock'. This is said to have been etched by Bodhidharma's features as he sat there, year after year. However, if an image is there, then it is recognizable only to someone who wants to see it. For others, it is simply a veined rock.

Shaolin Temple: Its Rise and Decline

In AD 574 Shaolin Temple suffered a reverse in its fortunes when Buddhism and Taoism were banned by royal decree of Emperor Wu Ti. The monastery was largely deserted and a handful of monks hid its relics and holy books until the decree was rescinded by the next emperor, Ching Ti. The reopened monastery was renamed Chi-hu, which meant 'Ascending The Hill'. It reverted to its original name around 682.

Originally, the monastery stood alone but as a result of successive land grants from the Sui and T'ang emperors, it soon grew into a prosperous complex of newly built buildings and productive agricultural land. This made it a target for repeated attacks by gangs of outlaws, thus providing an impetus to arrange for its own protection. During times of well-established secular administration, the monastery would have needed only to operate a small 'police force', but when law and order finally broke down, the need to protect the brotherhood of monks became paramount

18

and military training was stepped up. Despite this corps of warriors, the monastery was virtually razed to the ground during the latter part of the sixth century. Restoration began during the reign of Li Yuan (618–27), the first of the T'ang emperors and his beneficence established a close relationship between the temple and the state. This is perhaps one reason why the monks gave aid and support to his successor, Li Shi-min.

Patronage continued through the reigns of successive T'ang rulers, many of whom visited the temple. Accounts of their visits are still to be found in the inscriptions at Shaolin. Emperor Li T'sian established the rank of what he called 'Monks of Great Virtue'. This was to be conferred upon 10 persons only and in the event of a vacancy arising a replacement had to be selected from amongst the other monks.

Eventually, all this came to an end in the savage persecution of Buddhism under Emperor Wu-tsung in 845. A fanatical Taoist, determined to drive Buddhism from the shores of China, he began his persecution gradually in 844, with a tightening-up of supervision over the operation of Buddhist monasteries. This was followed by the persecution proper which closed smaller monasteries entirely and forced the younger monks to return to secular life. Holy images and books were destroyed and a contemporary account records how there were plans for 4,600 monasteries to be destroyed and 260,000 monks secularized. A further 40,000 Buddhist temples and shrines were to be destroyed and all lands belonging to Buddhists were to be confiscated. Fortunately, the persecution was brought to a premature halt by Wu-tsung's death during the following year. His successor revoked the edicts and Buddhism was spared further persecution.

Despite the pogrom's short duration, it succeeded in hitting Shaolin rather badly. Its lands were confiscated, the monks were dispersed, and the unattended buildings soon fell into disrepair. The returning monks found it dilapidated and were unable to raise the necessary capital to have it restored. In fact they had to wait 30 years before the temple was finally restored to it former glory.

Shaolin continued through both the Sung (960–1279) and Chin (1115–1234) Dynasties, each of which has left its mark in terms of pavilions and stelae.

The ensuing Yuan, Ming and early Ch'ing Dynasties all celebrated Shaolin as the home of Ch'an Buddhism, though it suffered badly at the hands of the Mongol invaders and had to be extensively rebuilt. Shortly after this latest renovation, the monastery was all but gutted by a serious fire and, this time, restoration work was not completed until well into the Ming Dynasty. Ming rule brought about a regularization of all Buddhist activity and required that head monks be appointed only through a royal decree. This regulation persisted into the Ch'ing Dynasty and grants of money were periodically made for construction of new buildings and renovation of old ones. The most important of these later projects was in 1735 and included the building of a single large dormitory to bring all the monks together. This had unfortunate local ecological effects in that the timber required was taken from a beautiful adjacent cypress grove, leaving it bare and treeless. It remains so to the present day.

The end of the Ch'ing Dynasty saw the temple on the decline once more. It was repeatedly attacked by bands of outlaws and subject to the depredations of greedy local administrations. Within the monastery too, things were on the decline. This showed itself in the breakdown of monastic discipline and ensuing disorder.

In 1928, the monastery was once again severely damaged by fire. Indeed, on this occasion, the fires burned so fiercely that they are claimed to have lasted 40 days. They completely destroyed three of the halls but fortunately left the temple proper and its murals unharmed. By now, the monastery was in a very poor state of repair. Its dilapidation increased during the Japanese occupation and it finally passed into the hands of the Chinese communists in 1949. The monks were treated as ordinary labourers and allowed to live off the land but their religious observances were frowned upon. Major restoration projects were financed by the central government in 1974 and 1979 and, comparatively recently, the monks have been allowed to continue with their devotions.

Shaolin Temple and the Martial Arts

What is it about Shaolin that made it into a legend as far as martial arts practice is concerned? How is it that a pacifist religion like Buddhism is able to involve itself in armed warfare? What forms of martial arts were practised at Shaolin? These three questions are the subject of this section. Taking them in the reverse order, we need to discover what systems were practised over the fourteen hundred-odd years of Shaolin's existence.

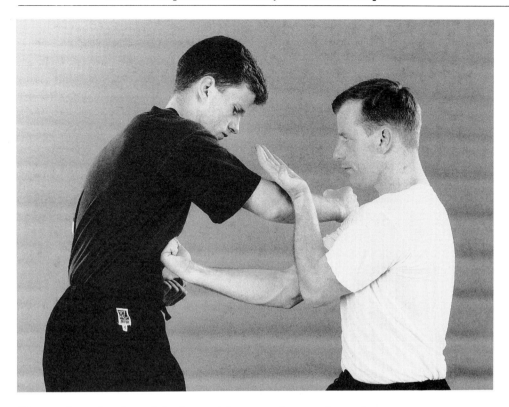

Unarmed combat is useful when neither party is armed, or when you wish to arrest someone without causing them mortal injury

Armed and Unarmed Combat

Some general points are relevant here. The first is that proficiency in unarmed combat is useful in a non-military situation but will not help on the battlefield, where the majority of combatants are armed. We know that Shaolin monks fought alongside regular troops and therefore we must conclude that they used weapons in their martial art. This is confirmed by reference to the later wall murals, which depict Shaolin monks practising with a variety of swords, spears, knives and staffs.

Unarmed combat is useful where no one else is armed, or where one combatant is unskilled in the usage of weapons. It is relevant to police duties, where you need to separate two rowdies who are brawling, rather than to kill them. Again, some of the wall murals depict monks fighting with their bare hands, so we can assume that unarmed combat certainly was taught.

21

What schools or styles of martial arts were taught at Shaolin? The quick answer to this is that many styles were taught there in 1,400 years. It is known that many criminals became monks – indeed this became one of the grounds for forcibly secularizing members of the community during the Great Persecution. Possibly some of the intake comprised ex-military men and these no doubt rendered good service when the monastery was under attack. They may well have provided a basis for instruction in the martial arts, to be built upon by those who came after. It is at least plausible that such may well have been the sources of what we might call 'house styles'. From time to time, new skills would be brought in when foreign monks visited, or when other military men took up the tonsure.

It is certainly wrong to make out that there was just one static style at Shaolin. Modern day experience shows how styles drift over the course of decades. So how much more could they change over the centuries as each successive grand master added his own interpretations to the shared core of knowledge. The least credible notion of all was that all martial development came from just one person – Bodhidharma – in the form of a series of exercises. Even when these alleged exercises are shown, they involve no weapons usage. Scarcely more credible is the legend concerning The Five Ancestors. These were five monks who remained alive after the temple was sacked, and each of them gave rise to a separate line of subsequent development.

One account of martial arts practice at Shaolin claimed that young monks practised the vigorous forms that we now refer to as 'external'; that is to say, using a deal of obvious muscle power. This satisfied their physical exuberance. What then happened was that as they grew older, they are thought to have taken up the 'internal' arts. The hidden assumption here is that, somehow, the external arts were no more than an initial stage that culminated in mastery of the internal arts. This is not the case. What is more likely is that as muscles became weaker and less elastic, so training shifted towards the more gentle expressions of martial art practice. The older man who has practised martial arts all his life will have acquired economical ways of moving that make his practice look deceptively relaxed. This theme is further developed in Chapter 3.

Five Animals Boxing (based on the movements of the tiger, the bird, the deer, the monkey and the bear) was developed from Hua Tuo's bodybuilding programme by the famous boxer, Bai Yu-feng. This, rather than the notion of The Five Ancestors, is

Methods of fighting with the stick were taught at Shaolin and 'Bodhidharma's walking sticks' was the name given to a system which used two together

thought to be the forerunner of modern-day systems of external Chinese martial art. Bai was also responsible for originating 18 postures to be take up in the sequence known as 'Invigorating The Muscles'. This is sometimes wrongly ascribed to Bodhidharma. The boxer Yu Fei subsequently refined this sequence into 'The Eight Graceful Movements' and these came to supplant the original as a basic exercise form for Shaolin monks. The original exercise persisted and gave rise to over 170 variant forms, some of which are still practised today.

23

The staff became the symbol of Shaolin martial art though the monks also used the single sword, double swords, the 'spring and autumn' swords, the 'plum blossom' swords and the spear. Single and double sticks were taught, the latter being known as 'Bodhidharma's walking sticks'. Odd weapons such as the nine-section whip, single whip and bladed rings were also part of the armoury. These weapons presented regular troops with a problem since they had been trained to deal only with orthodox military weapons. Unusual weapons therefore placed them at a considerable disadvantage. Life or death confrontations are the battlefield's form of natural selection. Effective strategies mean the inventor lives to teach his techniques.

The monks developed training forms based on successful combative effectiveness to teach proficiency in weapons usage. These forms consisted of a set number of movements to be performed in a certain order. Though these taught skill in weapons usage, they also improved the level of endurance and built up the body in exactly the right way for martial arts practice.

Various types of pole were used at Shaolin, including the iron staff. This fearsome weapon could only be employed effectively by the strongest monks and reports from the Ming Dynasty tell how the monks used their weighty staffs to great success against Japanese raiders.

There are no records of the monks ever using guns. Their military hardware seems to have stopped at the sword and spear stage. This is the point where skill in weapons usage is overturned by innate effectiveness of the weapon itself. Consider how long it takes to become accomplished at closing with an enemy over a variety of terrain and then engaging him in skilful swordplay. Then contrast this with the requirements involved in pointing a gun and pulling the trigger. In the first scenario, the skilled monks would be able to give a good account of themselves against a peasant uprising. In the second, a band of monks would simply be gunned down from a distance by a less skilled rabble armed with rifles. Therefore the pragmatic monk will give up weapons training, except perhaps as an ancillary to the main thrust of unarmed combat, though certain weapons – such as the staff – might be retained for use in non-military situations.

The prowess of the monks of Shaolin is well attested to but one wonders just how true is the claim that 13 or 14 monks defeated an entire rebel army. Even were the army to have been composed largely of cowardly rabble, it would still be difficult to swallow the account. More likely is the suggestion that the 'army' was no more than a particularly large armed band and the monks' attack upon it took the form of guerrilla hit-and-run incursions rather than a pitched battle.

Monks sometimes left Shaolin to go out into the world. Perhaps they would journey to other Ch'an masters for further study, or withdraw from the religious community to emulate Buddha. The latter route would be extremely arduous and called for sympathetic villagers prepared to extend a welcome along the traveller's way. There is some evidence to suggest that monks trained in martial arts did not simply leave the temple, but were first tested. The method of testing is not now known, though it is suggested that they were obliged to demonstrate their ability against a row of 36 wooden dummies in what was called 'The Wooden Figures Lane'. They may also have had to spar with Shaolin masters and once again, the figure of 36 engagements appears in ancient accounts. There is, however, no evidence to suggest that the monks were obliged to lift a red-hot iron cauldron out of their path with just their forearms!

A Pacifist Religion Produces An Effective Martial Art
It has been suggested that the monks were taught martial art as a means of counterbalancing the long periods of inactivity spent in meditation. There is possibly a specialized justification for this and we shall come to that in due course. However, taking the suggestion at its face value, if a physical activity is to be taken up solely for improving one's health, then why take up one which is based upon tactics and techniques for killing and injuring other people? Why not the Chinese equivalent of volleyball or ping pong?

The obvious answer to this is that throughout its long history, Shaolin has been subject to attack by armed bands and peasant uprisings, so if some physical activity is to be taken up, why shouldn't it be something that could be used to protect the monastery?

A more sophisticated reason might be the very nature of martial art itself. The Ch'an doctrine includes the belief that true enlightenment derives from a realisation that nothing is permanent, that all is suffering. By leaving go of all desires, wants and fears, the mind is left able to contemplate the true and illusory nature of reality. The most stringent test for this is whether one can leave go of one's desire for life; if one can fight to the death without anger or fear. Compare this picture with that of the person who is fearful, or overcome with anger. Such a person is not in full control of himself; he makes mistakes which can be exploited. The object may then have been to help the monk towards enlightenment by training him to meet the ultimate challenge with complete equanimity.

This brings us to the second question; that of how a pacifist religion like Buddhism could become associated with martial art. For did the Buddha not specifically warn monks against associating with the military and against taking another's life? The picture is perhaps easier to see if we relate it to the 'You shall not kill' commandment of the Jewish and Christian religions. Though these religions prohibit the taking of life, they nevertheless condone participation in a war which will ultimately benefit mankind; a case of the lesser versus the greater evil. So it is with Buddhism. Theoretically, the Buddhist may kill another, provided that to do so will save the person to be killed from the karmic consequences of his act. In practice, such a dispensation is allowed only for those who have reached the stage of becoming bodhisattvas. However, lesser mortals may yet kill to protect the Buddhist community and it is upon this 'self-defence' basis that Shaolin monks took part in armed warfare.

The Legend
The third and final question is why Shaolin should have become a martial art legend? The first answer is suggested by its proximity to dynastic capitals, so it was in contact with the ruling administration and close enough at hand to intervene when necessary. Its interventions, when they occurred, were both timely and opportune. Shaolin was successful both in its military campaigns and in the high profile way in which it helped potential benefactors. Secondly, Shaolin was often a rich temple; a prime target for the oppressed poor and robber bands. In times of civil unrest and weak authority, a skilled militia furnishes invaluable protection.

2 The Philosophy of Shaolin

As we saw in the previous chapter, Shaolin Monastery was a seat of Ch'an Buddhism. This is often overlooked by those who are interested solely in its involvement with Chinese martial arts. Bear in mind that the practice of such arts was incidental to its main reason for existence, i.e., the study of Ch'an Buddhism. This study produced a particular kind of philosophy which, in turn, affected the performance of martial art.

Nowadays, people learn martial art techniques and wrongly construe from that that they are practising martial art. This is not true. Martial art is both a mental and a physical discipline; one without the other produces an imbalance. Consider the case of the person who trains at his martial arts techniques until he can perform them all perfectly. Then he finds himself in an actual life or death situation and runs away because he is frightened! What use, then, is all that physical ability? Or what about the unskilled person who is completely unafraid of death and takes on a trained warrior, only to die uselessly in the process?

Most people take the view that the will to survive is one of the most powerful biological urges affecting us. So how might a person negate it? How could a warrior fight against superior odds, yet without fear for his own life? What is it that makes such a warrior claim 'Life or death – they are both the same'? We can describe such a person as a fanatic; so overcome with zeal that he is carried away on the tide of his emotions. This may provide an explanation for some instances, but what of the kamikaze pilot? Was he seeing through a haze of blood lust when he manipulated an aircraft onto a moving target? I think not. We might say that the pilot was mentally disturbed but if so, then there seems to have been an inordinate number of such crazy people. Might we conclude that the pilot woke up one morning and felt so depressed that he thought 'life just isn't worth living, so I might as well dive my plane into an enemy ship!'?

Clearly, violent passion, insanity and deep depression can lead people to negate their will to survive but what about those who are calm, rational and sane, yet who are capable of acting without regard for their own survival? If we admit that there are such people, and evidence seems to indicate this, then we are left with the possible conclusion that there might be some kind of mental training which, if embraced wholeheartedly, allows us to negate our will to survive, whilst otherwise retaining the trappings of rational and sane conduct. We know that Shaolin monks were able to act in this way, so what is it that enabled them to do so? The obvious answer must be – Buddhism!

From one point of view, Buddhism can be seen as a life-denying discipline. It starts from the supposition that life is full of suffering, caused by unrequited cravings. Everything is impermanent; life, personal relationships, possessions etc. Everything is hollow and without true substance. Even the personality is just an illusion, brought into seeming existence as a result of the cravings and desires – though one might well ask, what is it that the cravings are acting upon? Be that as it may, the way to escape this pointless travail is to give up all possessions and all relationships so you are not attached to anything in this world.

Buddhist monks could therefore have no possessions beyond the robe they wore and the begging bowl they carried. As we saw in the previous chapter, China's extremes of climate meant that shelter was required and so Buddhist monastic communities began. These were working, self-sufficient communities in which monks followed Buddhist thought whether at work in the fields, or when seated in meditation. The object in following this type of life was to obtain a true understanding of the way things really are, rather than how they appear to us to be. This true understanding comes through an insight known as 'enlightenment'.

Ch'an Buddhism

The Ch'an sect of Buddhism is interesting in that it makes little use of Buddhist scriptures to point the way to enlightenment. Instead, it teaches the devotee to set aside what we regard as a rational outlook. We make our way through life by means of reasoning based upon knowledge, because that is the way of the world of illusion in which we live. The real world, however, is that which is not shaped by our senses and consequently, our senses cannot appreciate it. Therefore to understand that which is beyond the rational, we must throw off our reason-inspired tunnel vision. To illustrate what is being said, consider the following from the Mumonkan:

Once the monks of the Eastern Hall were disputing about a cat. Nan-chuan, holding up the cat said, 'Monks, if you can say a word of Ch'an, I will spare the cat. If you cannot, I will kill it!' No monk could answer, so Nan-chuan finally killed the cat. In the evening, when Chao-chu came back, Nan-chuan told him of the incident. Chao-chu took off his sandal, placed it on his head and walked off. Nan-chuan said 'If you had been there, I could have saved the cat.'

The behaviour of Chao-chu is ludicrous and appears non-rational. This is the way of Ch'an. But how can we ignore what our rational mind tells us? How can we short-circuit, as it were, our reasoning mechanism? One way is to ponder over a *Kung-an* (riddle) that cannot be solved by the application of rational thought processes. An unsophisticated example of such a riddle is 'What is the sound of one hand clapping?' The teacher chooses the riddle to suit the student and great masters have helped students towards enlightenment simply by picking a riddle that is particularly suitable for the mind of the student to whom it is given. The student then reports back to the teacher on the results of his reflection.

Meditation

Meditation is common in Buddhism. Think of it as a psychic tool with which to examine the way the mind works. Meditation is an important part of Ch'an mental discipline, though it is not essential that it takes place in the seated position. Meditation can express itself through a skilled activity, where the body moves seemingly by itself and the mind is alert, yet tranquil. Obviously such a notion can be applied to martial art training and has led to that training being described as 'Moving Zen'.

However, the usual picture of meditation is that of the seated or kneeling monk, with back straight and hands resting on the thighs. The face is composed yet relaxed and breathing is regular, yet controlled. The tip of the tongue gently presses against the back of the front upper teeth. The eyes are narrowed and may concentrate upon a particular feature of the surroundings. The mind is stilled by concentrating upon a particular thing – such as a

Meditation is an essential part of Ch'an Buddhist practice though it need not necessarily take place in the kneeling position

kung-an – to the exclusion of all else. Sometimes, a restful image is conjured up in the mind. Floating in dark, cool water is excellent for this purpose because it is said to embody the element of *yin*, whereas thought energy is primarily of the competing *yang* species. The monk imagines the feel of the cool currents brushing against the body and gradually the mind becomes still.

Now this is a peculiar state for the brain to be in. Normally, brain activity is fast and furious during the waking state and during those periods of sleep known as REM (Rapid Eye Movement). Yet here we have a waking state and a relatively inactive brain. Electroencephalographs show that the meditating brain is producing alpha waves – a waveform that is normally seen only when the eyes are closed. But here it is happening when the eyes are open. It has been suggested that the energy which normally goes into producing our customary maelstrom of thoughts becomes available for other purposes, such as healing psychic scars and releasing tensions.

The meditating monk is calm, yet is aware of what is happening around him. His attention is unfocussed; he is aware of everything. If action is called for, then action is taken. Intensive physical training has taught the body how to execute even complex moves without the user having to think about which bit comes after what. The advancing spear point is therefore avoided without the need to consciously record the danger and choose the most appropriate response. There is no fear, there is no anger; there is nothing to slow the execution of martial art technique.

30

The Way to Enlightenment

The novice monks ask many questions but generally these are relatively pointless because unfortunately they don't actually know what real and necessary knowledge is. They think that by asking the teacher, they will obtain answers to help them attain enlightenment. What they do not realize is that enlightenment comes from within; it cannot be trained in from without! The enlightened monk asks only a few questions, and then only as a last resort when his own insight has not enabled him to find an answer. When voiced, these questions are not about superficial matters but reflect the depth of the monk's own true knowledge. By this, the master is able to gauge how far that monk is from enlightenment. A monk's true knowledge can also be assessed by his response to the master's questions. Consider the following discourse taken from the Keitoku Dentoroku between Bodhidharma and his disciples, shortly before he died:

Nine years had passed and he (Bodhidharma) now wished to return westwards to India. He called his disciples and said: 'The time has now come. Why doesn't each of you say what you have attained?'
The disciple Tao-fu replied: 'As I see it, the truth neither adheres to words or letters, nor is it apart from them. It functions as the Way.'
The master said: 'You have attained my skin.'
A nun, Tsung-chi'h said: 'As I understand it, the truth is like the auspicious glimpse of the Buddha land of Aksobhya; it is seen once but not a second time.'
The master said: 'You have attained my flesh.'
Tao-yu said: 'The four great elements are originally empty; the five skandhas have no existence. As I believe it, no Dharma can be grasped.'
The master said: 'You have attained my bones.'
Finally there was Hui-k'o. He bowed respectfully and stood silent.
The master said: 'You have attained my marrow.'

The dawning of enlightenment does not mean the end of Buddhist practices. Even the most enlightened Buddhist continues to meditate. As a result of training, the monk remains calm under the most stressful conditions, for there is no aggression in him; neither is there any self-doubt, since that is a block to further progress. The monk is expected to conduct himself with a quiet and natural dignity that has nothing to do with possessions; for whilst one might respect expensive clothes, one need not have any regard for the person wearing them. The monk's self-confidence is neither misplaced nor inappropriate. He doesn't compare himself with others but treats them as equals. Out of his gentleness comes real strength.

Whatever the monk does is performed with total dedication. His brain is active as he works and he constantly examines everything he does; for he may be doing something which he thinks is correct but it is not. And how could he discover this to be the case without constantly enquiring? Thus it is that the monk is totally dedicated, training in his own world and quite oblivious to what others are doing.

The Ch'an monk accepts criticism and praise with equanimity. He needs no external discipline because his own self-discipline is more rigorous. This natural discipline derives from his mental state and it is quite different from that which is imposed through external rules, laws and punishments.

The monks' teacher shows the Way in stages, lesson by lesson. For there is a right time and a right place to learn something. If too much is revealed too soon, then they might never come to fully understand it. Practice is made into a challenge that the monks must come to grips with and defeat. This challenge is both external and internal. The former develops the discipline needed to overcome the rigours of practice; the latter tests the monks' attitude to it.

The good teacher helps them to discover mistakes through their own examination because this is the only way to self-improvement. Indeed, ultimately it is all down to the student because the attainment of enlightenment is never conferred by anyone else, only the self. In conclusion, it could be argued that the way to enlightenment is made up of 25 per cent guidance from the teacher and 75 per cent effort from the monk. A failure to give that 75 per cent and the monk will never attain enlightenment.

The monk has the advantage of his teacher's knowledge, so in theory at least, he is capable of surpassing the latter. This does not mean, however, that he will simply become a clone of the master; since they are different people he will remain an individual. The master, like the Buddha, is no more than a signpost, pointing the way.

This, then, is the way of the Buddha, and the path by which the Shaolin monks were able to purge themselves of fear and attachment to self.

3 The Various Forms of Shaolin Kung Fu

This chapter will take the view that there is not, and never has been, one single form of Shaolin Temple kung fu, except in the sense that at any one time, there may have been a particular number of interpretations being practised.

When we look at the many styles of Chinese martial art being practised today, we see a bewildering array of interpretations on the basic theme of using the hands and feet to attack the opponent. There is a wide range of interpretation even within a single style, such that the extremes of one school eventually merge with the extremes of other schools. There is also a range of variation within a tradition that is related to the age of the headmaster. Thus, the comparatively young headmaster may favour certain tactics, techniques and stances but when he is older, other preferences come to take priority. From time to time, senior students may leave that headmaster to found their own schools within the same tradition, so the point in the headmaster's lifespan at which they leave will determine which interpretation of the tradition they carry away with them. This consideration is of relevance in view of the number of Shaolin monks who either left the temple to travel to other monasteries, or who left and then simply attached themselves to secular communities.

This, of course, is not the end of the matter. We would expect such variations to continue to take place throughout the tradition's long history. In theory, these changes must lead to a gradually widening divergence from the ancestral form, as subsequent headmasters inherit an ever more changed tradition. In practice, however, each tradition has wide but fairly distinct boundaries *within* which change takes place. That which occurs outside of the boundaries is not accepted by all the other senior members. Nevertheless, there is scope for considerable change even within a tradition with rigid designators, and yet more scope in those which are less rigidly defined.

If you do not accept these claims, then you are in effect asserting that the martial tradition is frozen at the moment of its origination and thereafter no development or change of any kind takes place in it. If you claim that what is now being practised in Shaolin Temple is the traditional system, then you must be in a position to demonstrate an unbroken line of succession reaching all the way back to T'ang China from the present day. For it is only by this means that you can show that there has always been and is now, one system that can be labelled *the* definitive Shaolin Temple martial art.

This position is impossible to hold. To take just one problem, we know that the temple has several times been razed and its monks scattered. Can we be so sure that the same combination of masters returned each time and took up where they left off? Much is said about the Five Ancestors but, regrettably, all of it is legend, with no supporting evidence.

Not surprisingly, I take the view that it is not possible to set down an unbroken line of succession and so we must allow that there may be a number of 'Shaolin systems,' each with a claim to authenticity. Thus, my opinion is that the only authenticity attaching to the present techniques taught in the temple is that they are being taught in the temple at the present time! Whilst that may perhaps validate one particular tradition, the problem remains that of distinguishing between those others with a legitimate claim and those without it.

One way of doing this is to look at a number of styles claiming Shaolin connections, to see whether they share any crucial characteristics. However, for these characteristics to be crucial, they must relate to non-practical aspects of the tradition. Thus, we cannot say that using a fist validates a claim to Shaolin ancestry, since the fist is a body weapon common to any system of fighting, whether Chinese or not. Could use of the pole in a martial art system be said to indicate a Shaolin connection? The answer to this must also be 'no', since people have been hitting each other with sticks since the dawn of time, and many non-Chinese fighting systems have used the quarterstaff. Then is there something peculiar about the Shaolin pole itself that the poles of other systems do not have? Again, the answer is 'no'. This must show, I think, that the notion of validating claims according to crucial characteristics is not straightforward.

The Internal Way and the External Way

The starting point for any consideration of Chinese martial art is the recognition of *nei chia* (the internal way) and *wai chia* (the external way). There is some evidence to suggest that despite their different origins, both forms were practised at Shaolin. In fact, one historical source claimed that monks at Shaolin first learned the external systems but later, when they became skilled at these, they

External martial arts are characterized by the obvious application of strength. Note the rictus of the face and the rigid forearm

began over again in the internal styles. Despite that, it is certainly a fact that Shaolin Temple Boxing has become better known for its external forms than its internal ones. But before considering these various claims, we may perhaps care to reflect upon the essential differences between the two ways. Thus we can take external systems to be those which use obvious muscle action to power techniques. The source of their effectiveness is seen by studying the action of the body in terms of physical dynamics:

● one muscle relaxes as the opposing muscle contracts;

● the contracting muscle is prestretched first to load it with energy, in the manner of an elastic band;

● the body moves behind the limb, so as to inject moving body weight into the equation;

● the muscles of the whole body contract on impact, forcing air from the lungs in a staccato grunt – such as one gets when heaving a heavy weight.

All of these are easily understandable principles; there is nothing magical or incomprehensible about them.

Contrast this with the internal way where the punch flies out without obvious muscle action propelling it – yet it is powerful all the same. Legends in the effectiveness of such systems as 'Great Ultimate Fist' describe how an apparently light touch from the master sent an exponent backwards, both feet literally off the ground. And attempts to unbalance the master merely caused the opponents to fall over!

These same feats are demonstrated today by *tai chi* masters but we now realise that they too are based upon purely mechanical principles – though less obvious than those of the external systems. For example, a sharp rap on the opponent's chest will produce an involuntary and explosive contraction of the psoas muscles, thrusting the arms and legs forward and throwing the person backwards. Note that the person flies backwards through the evoked action of his own muscles, not through the power of the applied punch. Similarly, some of the demonstrations of balance and the so-called 'unbendable arm' have been shown to be based upon simple triangulation of applied force – so the opponent is literally pushing against himself. The internal systems derive from

Internal martial arts use an apparently relaxed and flowing action in which great muscular effort is not apparent

Taoist principles and involve a naturally occurring energy known as *chi*. But if Shaolin was a Buddhist temple and Taoism another religion, how is it that internal systems could have found their way into the temple – if indeed they did? There are two possible answers to this. The first is that we do not know for sure whether the monks of Shaolin did, in fact, practise a true form of internal martial art. It could simply have been that the older and most

37

Some masters of tai chi are able to make their opponents literally fly backwards with the lightest of blows

skilled monks had developed economy of movement, precision of target-attack and timing to the extent that their external system appeared effortless and flowing, much like an internal system.

Is this a valid form of internal martial art? Or is it simply a detuned form of external martial art? The question is not so easy to answer because when we examine the adapted techniques, we see that the fast-accelerating punching arm is replaced by a slower and shorter thrust that acts through the body's centre of gravity. So it seems like the actual techniques themselves have been significantly modified – perhaps to the extent that we might now regard them as internal.

An alternative and simpler explanation could have been that Shaolin monks actually did practise an internal system brought in from Taoist sources. This is not a risky supposition to make since, by and large, early Buddhism and Taoism coexisted in relative harmony. A prestigious monastery like Shaolin would have attracted a large number of martial arts teachers, so many different styles no doubt met and mingled there during the temple's long history. Some of these masters would have been from the external styles, others might have come from internal styles.

Basic Principles of the Martial Arts

Regardless of whether it is internal or external, what are the characteristics of a skillfully applied martial art? The following are offered as a basis for discussion. We can begin by saying that the skilled practice of martial art involves only such movement as is necessary to accomplish one's aim. Thus, the opponent's attacking punch is diverted only as much as is necessary to make it miss. Constant fidgeting and unnecessary moving about is replaced by a watchful calm that detects attacks even as they are about to begin.

The less skilled martial artist bats an incoming punch to one side and then uses a counter. The master goes out to meet an attack, continuing his block through, but changing it into a strike. Economy dictates that since the blocking arm was closer to the target, why not use it also as the basis for an immediate counter? It is true that the arm is already partly extended and therefore has a shorter distance over which to act, but this shortcoming is remedied by a slight forward shift of the centre of gravity that adds body weight to the strike's power. The unskilled counter is made with a full fist, whereas the expert strikes with just one knuckle, so force is concentrated over a smaller area.

The basic method of throwing a long-hand punch uses energy derived from a strong pull-back of the non-punching arm. The punch is thrust out on the end of an actively extending arm as the other withdraws, and the muscles tighten at the expected moment of impact, giving momentary general rigidity and conferring effective recoil-absorbtion. By comparison with this, the skilled man simply throws his fist at the target – it does not matter what the other hand is doing. Power is generated not so much by muscular effort as by shifting the bodyweight forwards, so the shoulders become rounded as the punch extends. This shrugging action is most important and we shall have more to say about it later. The fist and forearm clench momentarily on impact and then immediately relax again. But do not confuse this final muscle action with the whole-body focus of the less skilled martial artist. Here, muscle 'lock-up' is localized in the lower forearm and fist, making the latter seem heavier and more dense. The rest of the body is completely relaxed, so it can move quickly in any direction.

The experienced martial artist has a low rate of technique redundancy. This means that if he throws two techniques, then both will hit their target. He does not fire techniques like bullets from a machine gun, hoping that one at least will hit something.

The master uses the twin aspects of stance and guard to judge the standard of others. Many students can develop power but are thrown off-balance when they are attacked. Or, the opponent moves away quickly and the student fails to follow, so the initiative passes from him. The skilled exponent stands seemingly relaxed, but his centre of gravity has been lowered so he is better able to resist the pressure of attack. He turns his body square-on to the opponent, so he can channel his energy effectively. His movements are quick and made without hesitation. The less skilled student moves only once the opponent has advanced but then it is too late.

The skilled exponent's guard is not rigid because strength does not reside in rigidity. Instead his guard is resilient, and does not give way easily to pressure. However, when the pressure against him becomes too great, he suddenly shifts, so the energy of attack is diverted and the opponent's own power is used to open him up to an immediate and effective counter.

Skill is therefore the refuge of the experienced martial artist and serves to maintain an advantage against younger and stronger opponents.

4 Power Delivery in Shaolin Systems

The point has already been made that there is no single system of Shaolin Temple Boxing. Accordingly, this chapter will review various methods of power delivery found in the major divisions of Chinese martial art. The following, therefore, are general comments applicable to all forms of Shaolin practice:

1. Paradoxically, strong students are sometimes at a disadvantage because their very strength makes their movements jerky and stiff. Their movements may look powerful but they are actually spasmodic and weak. It is essential to move smoothly, with energy flowing throughout the technique and not just during the muscle spasms which typically accompany the beginning and end of movements. The whole body must link in and correctly augment the critical actions, otherwise they will possess only local energy. Local energy is developed only in the striking limb and, though impressive, it is never as powerful as the energy developed by whole-body actions.

2. Energy must be conserved by using relaxed movements so it becomes possible to train for longer periods. Having said that, the energy is always there, even if it is not active at any particular moment. Think of it as potential energy, available for instantaneous use.

3. The concept of the centre-line of the body – whether yours or the opponent's – lies at the core of Chinese martial art. It is widely believed that techniques delivered through the centre-line are more powerful than those which are not. Thus it is that the Chinese divide the body into four gates. The lower inside gates extend up the line of the body from groin to mid-chest. The upper gates extend from chest to the head. The outside gate equivalents lie beyond the body and head. Any technique, be it block, punch

41

Chinese martial artists divide the opponent's body into the four 'gates'. The inside gates follow the limits of the body, the outside gates extend beyond this

Right: The person on the left has allowed his hands to cross his own centre-line, so his posture is weak. The man on the right has kept his hands to their respective sides of the centre-line

or strike, which crosses the centre-line will lose whole-body power, though it may retain local power. If it is not possible to deliver a technique through the centre-line because you are at an angle to the target, then turn your whole body until the hips and shoulders are facing the correct direction.

4.   Energy of impact depends upon a number of factors, two of which are acceleration and mass. The smaller and lighter body weapon must travel very fast indeed to match the energy of impact of a slower moving but more massive weapon. In practice, this means that the fast-moving lightweight may have to strike five times in order to achieve the same total effect as a single blow from the slower heavyweight. So if you are both lightly built and agile, then you should train to deliver a series of fast strikes. If, on the other hand, you weigh 90 kilos or more and are very strong, then train to deliver a smaller number of sledgehammer blows. Choose the most suitable alternative for your build.

Long-hand Boxing

Having dealt with these general points, we turn now to a consideration of some of the major types of Chinese martial art.

Long-hand boxing styles typically begin with a punch from the 'cocked' position. The left fist is drawn back to the hip; the right is fully extended and the palm is open

The first type to be considered are the long-hand boxing schools (e.g. *chang chuan* and *choy li fut*). These are so named because they use the full length of the arm to deliver a punch or strike (a punch is a blow delivered with the hand closed into a fist, a strike is a blow in which the hand is open). Typically, the first is 'cocked' prior to punching. This is to say, it is drawn back from the eventual target and the elbow is flexed. The other arm may be extended forward as a guard. The shoulders are relaxed and do not hunch up.

44

The punching fist travels all the way from the hip to the target

A typical practice position might be horse stance, with the feet spread by a pace-and-a-half and the knees forced open. The back is upright and the backside is tucked in. The knees are directly above the feet. The cocked fist is palm-upwards facing on the hip, the extended fist is turned palm to the floor. The best way to visualize the punching action is to imagine a rope passing from the extended fist, around a pulley and back to the cocked fist so when one moves, the other has no option but to follow at the same speed and over the same distance. The extended arm is drawn back strongly,

45

so the cocked fist moves an equal distance from the hip at an equal speed. Both fists rotate as they reach the limit of their respective movements and both come to a stop at exactly the same time. The arms are quite relaxed during the movement but the punching fist tightens spasmodically as it nears the imaginary target. This makes the fist into a dense weapon, capable of causing injury to whichever part of the opponent's body that it strikes. Note that the muscle contraction is restricted to those which make the fist. The involvement of any other muscles will simply slow the punch.

Not all long-hand punches are linear; some follow a circular path. These punches tend to be the most powerful of all, since the muscles can act on the limb over a considerable distance, and the mechanism of the punch means that it is not limited by elbow extension. Despite the curving path, circular punches use the same type of pulley action as that previously described, with one fist cocked and the other extended forward. The leading fist withdraws as the other swings over and around in an action similar

Above: Shift body weight forward and throw your punch; using the pulley effect of the withdrawing left arm to help power it

Left: Curving punches are probably the most powerful of all hand techniques, though they travel a great distance and can be both recognised and countered from an early stage. Here, the punching fist is pulled right back

to overarm bowling. Body weight moves onto the front foot during the latter part of the delivery and there is a fair degree of forward lean.

Though this punch is tremendously powerful, it provides some fairly obvious cues, so the skilled opponent can take steps to avoid it. On the other hand, its circular path makes it very difficult to block and it is apt to curl around a deflecting hand and continue on into the target. Sometimes the sheer power of the technique is enough to sweep the opponent's guarding hand away altogether.

Short-hand boxing throws the heavy fist a short distance into the target. Here the fist is only a foot or so away from the opponent's face when the punch is performed

Short-hand Boxing

Short-hand boxing (e.g. Wing Chun Kuen) relies upon quite different principles to accelerate the fist into the target. The idea of localized muscle power is here carried to an extreme and training consists of making the fist as dense as possible. The exponent of short-hand boxing might well comment that it takes only a light blow with a sledgehammer to cause injury! Rigorous training in these systems allows the exponent to strike effectively from any angle, so stance and body positioning become less important.

The first requirement of the short punch is to close the fist

The arm is accelerated by a shrugging action of the shoulders. The fist tightens sharply on impact

tightly to exclude air from it. This must be achieved by tensing only the muscles of the forearm, leaving the elbow free and the shoulder relaxed. Beginners thrust the fist out instead of throwing it at the target. This changes the whole dynamics of the punch and makes it into a long-hand technique. But if it then strikes home, the rigid arm and unsuitable stance fail to absorb recoil and the exponent is knocked backwards. Note that the fist is not contracted until impact is imminent. At first it tilts forward on the wrist but then it straightens sharply as it contracts. The elbow and shoulder joints are relaxed, so limb-speed is not slowed.

49

Additional power can be generated by moving the centre of gravity forward, in support of the punching action

Additional power is produced through contraction of the pectoral muscles on the front of the chest. This moves the shoulders sharply forward behind the punch and adds body weight to the power of the extending arm. Like the closing of the fist, this shrugging action must be made as quickly as possible.

Still more power can be generated by moving the centre of gravity behind the punch. This is done either with a slight forward movement of the leading foot or by moving the hips imperceptibly forward and up. Even a light person generates energy when he moves quickly enough and the distance covered is less important than the acceleration.

The punch must not be focused with the intention of generating maximum impact at a particular point, for though this may feel powerful, it really is not. The trick is to try and strike through the target, relying on impact rather than muscle action to bring the blow to a stop. A good way to visualize it is to think of a golfer's swing. Does the club come to an immediate stop once it hits the ball? Follow-through is an essential component of good form. Also, note that there may be a slight pulley action in the classic short-hand punch, though an equal and opposite movement definitely does not take place.

Quite a different set of principles power a third type of short punch. This begins from a cocked position on the hip, with the leading hand opened into a guard position. This time there is a fully coordinated pulley action, with the leading hand pulling back exactly as the punch moves forward. However, the fists do not rotate and impact is made with the palm of the fist pointing upwards. Note that the punch is made into the centre-line of the body, using relaxed shoulders and a slight forward movement of the punching hip. The punching elbow is kept close to the ribs so it harnesses the user's centre of gravity. A slight forward movement of both hips adds further power. Sometimes the pulley action is abbreviated when the guarding hand curls around the back of the opponent's neck and draws his head forward, down, and onto the punch.

Kicking

Kicking techniques also use straight and circular actions. The kicking leg possesses a great deal of energy by virtue of its weight, and the faster the leg muscles can be contracted, the more powerful the kick becomes. All parts of the foot are used, though the heel and sole of foot are the most common. Martial art systems said to have arisen in the north of China typically use more kicks than southern Chinese systems. The latter tend to close distance to the point where kicks above the level of the opponent's waist are dangerous to the user. Northern forms tend to fight from a greater distance, keeping out of the opponent's range until an opportunity comes to use a long-ranging kick.

Kicks generally use a stamping action. The foot is drawn up and the kicking knee is brought in close to the body. Then the lower leg is thrust out and down into the opponent's groin or knee with the foot held vertical, or inclined to one side or the other. Sometimes

Southern Shaolin kicks are used from short distances and are seldom used against targets above the opponent's waist

the hips are brought forward behind the action, though you should never lean back since this causes poor recoil absorption. One type of kick is delivered with the body turned sideways-on, or away from the opponent. Despite the change in body angle, the mechanism of the kick is the same. Sometimes a slight turning hip action is used, in which case the instep travels diagonally forward and up, into the opponent's groin, or to the inside of his thigh or knee.

Power Generation

External systems of Chinese Boxing often use a shout or grunt to signify the fusion of body and mind into the technique being applied. This sound comes from the diaphragm rather than the lungs and is like that which occurs during any strenuous muscular exertion such as lifting a heavy weight. The air literally explodes out as the muscles of the body contract during the technique. This, of course, will not happen when local energy only is used.

Internal systems use no obvious system of power generation yet

52

Northern Shaolin kicks are more flamboyant and are often aimed at the opponent's head

they appear to be extremely powerful. It is claimed that they make use of a natural form of energy which flows through the body and which can be used to power a technique. Interesting though this suggestion is, there is no reason to believe it because the sometimes spectacular effects of internal punches and strikes can be simulated by purely physical principles.

The first point to bear in mind is that the relaxed limb travels faster and accelerates harder than one that is tense. This is obvious when one thinks about it since limb speed is not only governed by how quickly a set of muscles can contract, but also by how quickly the opposing muscle set can relax. As was mentioned at the beginning of this chapter, strong people often appear very powerful but this is only because their muscles bulge with the effort of overcoming equally strong competing muscles. If it were possible to more fully relax the muscular antagonists to an action, then theoretically at least it should be possible to punch quickly yet without a great deal of muscular effort.

Thus the internal systems throw a punch like someone lobbing a brick. The arm is relaxed and the fist sails into the target at a

53

The kicking knee is brought high, then the heel is thrust downwards into the opponent's knee

surprising speed. Such things as body orientation are secondary and power is generated from any position – making the art extremely versatile as well as effective. The fist contracts briefly on impact and then immediately relaxes again, so it can be withdrawn quickly and used again. Sometimes the body moves behind the punch, though without the spasm and urgency of the external systems. The effect of this is to add kinetic body mass. It also seems that internal stylists have a wide knowledge of the body's vital points so even a punch of diminished energy can generate a disproportionate effect.

Hierarchy of the Systems

Finally, as we noted in the last chapter, it is tempting to assign an order of sophistication to the various systems which may have been taught in the temple. You will recall that one historical source claimed that monks first learned and became expert in the external systems before beginning their final study, which was of the internal systems. Whether this assertion is true cannot now be proven though it does seem to be in accord with the natural tendency to place internal systems on a higher plane of sophistication than the external arts. Read again the previous chapter, in which it is suggested that some of the internal arts may have come from the way older external stylists practised. Even if we accept that the internal arts are very advanced, this does not necessarily mean that the external arts are not sophisticated – because they undoubtedly are. Perhaps we can say that they are as sophisticated in their own way as are the internal systems.

A similar stamping action is used for sideways-facing kicks

5 Methods of Shaolin Fitness Training

Before launching into details of practice it is as well to spend a short time looking at the exercises which we believe may have been used by the Shaolin monks. It is probably wrong to regard their training as being similar to that practised nowadays. For example, there is no evidence to show that they were aware of the benefits of a warm-up or a cool-down. Indeed, there is little evidence at all to show that exercises of any kind were performed! It may well have been the case that simple practice of martial art made the monks fit enough, without recourse to additional training. Yet we do know of early exercise systems that appear to have been studied at Shaolin – for example, the Five Animals exercise of Dr Hua Tuo. These used what was thought to be the 'essence' of each particular animal's grace and strength.

It is said that Bodhidharma also taught two exercises, sometimes translated by the curious titles 'washing the marrow' and 'exchanging the sinews'. It may well be that he did, since it is not impossible that, being an Indian, he knew something of yoga. However, it is less likely that these exercises, if indeed they ever existed, were used as the basis for the development of martial art systems. Could one develop a fighting system from aerobics? But before abandoning Bodhidharma's role as founder of either exercise system or martial art, one might wish to conclude that if he was the son of a noble family, then he may well have practised martial art. Though wholly unsubstantiated, this is at least comprehensible and it may well explain the persistent legends about Bodhidharma's involvement with martial art practice.

It is also worth pointing out that Bodhidharma was a highly esteemed patriarch from the mother country of Ch'an Buddhism. It is therefore probable that any instruction he gave the Shaolin monks would have been highly regarded. But whether or not Bodhidharma taught exercises to the Shaolin monks, other exercise systems certainly were known to them.

Health as Opposed to Fitness

These exercises bear absolutely no relationship to the 'external' exercises practised in the West. For example, the Chinese tend to stress the notion of health, rather than that of fitness. We often confuse these two and say that if a person can run a long distance very quickly, then that person is healthy. This is not always the case because it may well be that the runner has high cholesterol, or a stone in his kidney – yet he is nevertheless fit to run. So it is possible to be fit to achieve some purpose, yet not be what we would regard as healthy. This distinction is important when considering the Chinese notions of fitness and exercising. As a partial aside, even the notion of 'fitness' is specific insofar as a weightlifter might well be fit enough to press a great weight, yet be completely unfit in the matter of flexibility.

So when we use the term 'fitness', what we actually mean is that people can train themselves to become fit to perform a particular activity. This is quite different from the whole body health which interests the Chinese. Indeed, their objective in using exercises is to become fit for life!

The traditional Chinese view is that the best type of fitness programme for martial arts practice is the martial art itself; for whereas the various fitness routines undoubtedly improve strength, endurance and suppleness, they seldom produce exactly the right kind of improvement. The body responds to training so you gradually become able to work harder over longer periods and, after six months, most of the initial problems will have cleared. Indeed, any attempt to hurry natural adaptation will, the Chinese believe, bring about a premature *fitness* which does nothing to improve health and may actually harm it.

Exercising for health is important because hard martial art training can only be undertaken by a healthy person. Someone with osteoarthritis of the knees, for example, will not be helped by practising kicks. If the body is ill, then much of its energy is diverted to coping with the illness and insufficient remains to supply the demands of training. Therefore make the body healthy before beginning martial art training.

Mind and Body

Chinese exercises aim not just at producing a healthy body, but at producing a healthy mind integrated with a healthy body; for, as I remarked earlier, what is the use of a skilful warrior who is also a coward or a bully? Therefore all Chinese exercises involve a degree of mental training. This is not to increase your intelligence, rather it aims to balance your mind – for the term 'mental imbalance' that we Westerners use is taken very seriously by the Chinese. They knew about psychosomatic disorders a long time before western doctors gave them credence.

The Chinese have long recognized that the mind is the seat of conflict and contradictions which, in their working out, may produce symptoms which are completely unrelated to the actual cause. Think of a house with a fire in the basement. Smoke is trapped within the building, gradually fills all its rooms and eventually escapes from the eaves. But is there a fire in the roof? No, it is in the basement. This analogy applies to the Chinese concepts of mind – body interaction; i.e., the mind is disturbed so the body aches! Rubbing liniment on the ache will not take away its cause.

By means of the correct training, you will be able to train your mind, so these conflicts are processed and balanced from within. The effects could, I suppose, be likened to hypnotism. The skilled hypnotist is able to penetrate to the root of a mental problem and bring it to the surface of the patient's mind, where it can be analysed and processed. In general terms, proper mental training does the same except that here, the identification of the problem is not done by a third party.

Meditation and Health

'One must polish the mirror of one's own mind,' the Chinese sages say, 'for only then will it reflect clearly.' Our normal state of consciousness reflects indistinctly, because the surface of the mind's mirror is dulled by a grime that is the ego. The ego develops as we mature, walling us off from others in order to protect itself from a hostile outer world. Through meditation, we hope to return to the original state of mind, known to the Chinese as the *sien tien*. This form of consciousness contains no hatred, fear, or aggression. It is without any kind of conflict or division, so the body can act freely and without interference. The question is then posed, how to polish the mirror of the mind? The answer is to use meditation, for a tranquil mind achieves clarity more quickly than a disordered mind.

As noted in Chapter 2, electroencephalogram read-outs show

that the amount of activity in the brain's cerebral cortex is reduced during meditation. Indeed, the level of activity appears to be lower even than during REM sleep and, nowadays, most psychologists appear to agree that meditation is effective at reducing anxiety and arousal.

The Chinese maintain that when the central nervous system is relaxed, everything functions without interference and energy floods through the body. Indeed, many meditators do report feeling a sense of warmth, or a tingling in the hands or feet. One suggestion is that this happens because the circulation is not being interfered with by nervous impulses, so the bloodvessels dilate, allowing a greater flow of blood through the body.

There are striking similarities between physical and mental training. For example, you may initially find it hard to lift a 20-kilo weight ten times but, after a little practice, you become able to do it easily. This is because your body has become accustomed to the task. However, increase the weight lifted and once again you will feel tired. So it is with meditation. At first it is very difficult to meditate but, as you persevere, so it becomes easier.

Extending the time spent in meditation brings about a return to those difficult first sessions, yet, as you persevere, meditation becomes easy again. Meditation seems to lead to a decrease in anxiety and nervous tension so eventually you will become capable of tolerating high levels of stress. One suggestion as to why this should be is that meditation has filled a reservoir of mental energy which can then be drawn upon as required.

As you probably know, there are various forms of meditation which can be performed whilst standing, sitting or lying down. In fact posture doesn't matter at all as long as you relax and keep your back absolutely straight. Breathing, however, is important; never hold your breath, or use strenuous breathing techniques. Instead you must relax the muscles in your chest, and the body's organs will relax too. Breathe naturally and do not take deep breaths to expand your chest. When you are fully relaxed, most of the breathing action is performed by the diaphragm muscle. You will see that your stomach expands as the diaphragm fills the lungs with air. Then it flattens as you exhale.

Visualize something in your mind as you meditate. It may be the sound of a word repeated over and over, quietly to yourself. If so, then time your thinking of the word to your exhalations to institute a natural rhythm. Alternatively, think of a soothing image – perhaps of waterfalls or rainbows. Whichever you choose, sit and contemplate it, narrowing your attention down to the visualization. You can meditate without visualizing anything at all. Simply watch the thoughts come and go in your mind, as though you were separate from them. This latter form of meditation is most likely to be that practised by the monks of Shaolin since it does not involve a narrowing-down of the consciousness. Indeed, that could prove positively fatal on the battlefield!

Though meditation is generally thought of as involving no movement, it need not be so. In fact you should become able to meditate as you perform the daily activities of life – whatever they might be. The Shaolin monks extended the sphere of their meditation into martial art training so it produced a calm yet watchful mind which was able to see techniques and opportunities, but was not hung-up on fears or anxiety.

Above: Lean forward and gather the imaginary flowers to you

Right: Straighten up and lean back, allowing the flowers to fall

Exercise in Conjunction with Meditation

Many other traditional Chinese exercises survive to this day, especially those originating from the Taoist traditions. They must each be performed whilst the mind is relaxed and meditating upon a particular mental image. Indeed, this visualization is as important as the exercise itself, and, without it, what remains of the exercise is of little value. Here are some exercises you can try.

The first one to consider uses the visualization of gathering flowers, then letting them fall. Begin by leaning forward and crossing your arms in front of your chest – as though collecting a large bundle of flowers. Straighten up and shift your weight back onto the rear leg, such that the sole of the leading foot rises. Open your arms wide. Then lean forward once more to collect the

61

Push forward with both hands. Then draw back, returning both hands to your sides

flowers. Breathe out as you spread your arms wide. Perform this exercise ten times.

To perform the second exercise, step forward with your right foot and execute a pushing move with both palms. Do not let your elbows splay out. Then draw back your weight onto the rear foot and pull both arms back to your sides, rotating the hands palm-downwards. Visualize that you are working with a partner who alternately draws you forward and pushes you back; you are responding to his muscular effort, rather than generating effort of your own. Breathe out as you push forwards and in as you draw

62

Twist your upper body and reach behind you

back. Repeat the exercise ten times.

Then face the front, extending both arms with fingers pointing. Twist your body to the right and look behind you. Pause, then twist your body fully to the left. Repeat this exercise five times on each side, breathing out as you turn to the right and in as you turn to the left. Visualize that you are passing a ball to a person standing immediately behind you.

Extend your arms above your head and bring the thumbs and index fingers of both hands together. Tilt your head back and look through the gap you have made. Keep thrusting upwards with

63

Straighten your arms above your head and look upwards

both hands as you lean; first to the right, then to the left. The leaning movement is slow and smooth and you should visualize yourself following the path of the sun across the sky. Breathe out as you lean away from centre, inhale as you move towards centre. Repeat the exercise five times on each side. Vary this exercise by circling your body from the waist, first in one direction, then in the other.

Bring the tips of your fingers together, turning your hands

64

Lean your body first to one side, then to the other

palm-upwards at the level of your stomach. Breathe in as you raise the hands smoothly to the height of your chin. Then twist them palm-downwards, breathing out as you return them to the starting position. This is an excellent deep-breathing exercise in which you should use your diaphragm as much as possible. Repeat the exercise ten times whilst holding a soothing picture in your mind.

As you can see, traditional Chinese exercises work the body gently and are suitable for all ages. The visualization plays an

Breathe in as you raise your palms

important part and serves to soothe the mind even as the body is being gently worked. From this state of tranquil attention, you are then ready to begin studying traditional Shaolin martial art.

6 Shaolin Stances and Movements

Perhaps the most eloquent display of the effectiveness of Shaolin stances and movements took place not all that long ago in Hong Kong. A senior British martial artist from an especially rigorous Japanese discipline went there in search of traditional training and after a series of refusals, he finally found a teacher who was at least prepared to listen to him. 'Show me what you can do', ordered the teacher, so the would-be student gave a display of technique. At the end of this, the master commented 'You are very good at what you do. What do you think I can teach you?' Fortunately, the student was not a fool and replied 'You may be able to teach me something that is more efficient!' This pleased the teacher who took him in as a student but not before demonstrating the efficacy of his own system. He selected a frail senior student of about 50 years of age and invited this young bull of a European to spar with him.

At first, the British chap felt constrained to avoid hurting his partner but he needn't have bothered. Every punch, kick, or rush forward met with nothing! The senior student simply moved just out of range and touched his opponent lightly on parts of the body the latter now knows to be vital areas.

The moral of this story is that mastery over distance and timing is a great skill to acquire and, once acquired, it puts you in the position of not being vulnerable to the opponent's attacks whilst being able to strike him at will. This is obviously very important if you have a slight build and the opponent is much stronger and heavier. However, it should be pointed out that mastery over distance is not something which can be applied when you are attacked in a telephone booth! This skill therefore leaves you with some limitations at least, so it is unwise to put all your eggs in just one basket.

Interestingly, the application of distance and timing seem nowadays to have dropped in importance in comparison with power and aggression. Indeed, many martial art schools seem overly concerned with simply getting in there and hitting the opponent hard! Such schools should take note of the story that introduced this chapter.

Stances

It is easy to be thrown off by some of the varied and fantastic poses taken up in modern Chinese martial art practice today. However, be all that as it may, martial art poses fall into four broad types. The first type is what we might call *ritual stances*. These are stances of respect, one example being the attention stance; when the teacher addresses the class, everyone takes up an attitude of polite attention. Typically this is an erect stance with the feet close together and the hands flat against the front of the thighs. Stances which show respect usually include an open hand clasping the fist, or the simple Buddhist greeting of holding the palms of the hands together in a prayerful attitude before the face. Quite obviously these have no martial significance beyond that described.

The second category of stance is what could be called *practice postures*. These are stances taken up to facilitate the execution of a particular type of technique. Thus a horse stance is used in the long-hand forms while the cat stance is taken up during practice with the pole. In both cases, the stance itself serves a secondary function. This is the case with most stances, i.e., they are not ends in themselves. Think of them as platforms from which the techniques of Shaolin kung fu are executed. Some techniques require highly specialized platforms, others do not. In fact there are those platforms which have no apparent function at all.

Consider a low horse stance, adopted when there is no opponent to respond to. Why should one remain for long periods of time in this rather exhausting position? The obvious answer is that it teaches you the feel of the correct stance, so you can adopt it as and when necessary during sparring. The less obvious answer is that it puts the muscles of the upper legs into tension, strengthening them in a particular way. A spin-off of this is that the strengthened muscles help to locate the knee joint, making it less prone to injury during kicking practice.

Top: Horse stance is used a great deal in the long-hand styles

Bottom: Cat stance withdraws the body from attack

68

The typical fighting stance is unpolarised, being neither too wide, too narrow, too short, too long, too high, or too deep. It allows the widest variety of movements to be made

The third category of stances is what we might regard as *medium-term postures*. These are the 'on-guard' positions taken up prior to launching an attack or making a defence. Typically they are unpolarized. That is to say, the body's weight is distributed evenly between the feet. One foot leads the other and they are about a shoulder width apart, so both latitudinal and longitudinal stability is conferred. An average stance is short enough to permit an explosive advance but long enough to allow you to 'dig in' under the opponent's furious assault. We can say that it allows fast movement in any direction whilst conferring an effective guard.

70

'Crane-on-a-rock' stance looks flamboyant when posed in this manner but actually it is held only for fractions of a second

The fourth type is what we might call *transient stances*. These are the highly unusual and sometimes flamboyant postures taken up for instants of time as one is withdrawing from the opponent, or retrieving a technique. A typical stance of this type might be the crane-on-a-rock posture (crane stance) in which the exponent stands with one knee raised high and both arms outstretched. This is virtually useless against a committed attacker but, then, it is not intended to be used in that case. Here the exponent has withdrawn from the opponent's attack and is poised just before delivering a fast counter-attack.

71

Stances used in sparring have a number of points in common. They all allow the exponent to be in the right place at the right time, with the right body weapon already cocked. They prevent him from being caught out on the wrong foot and ensure that all movements are agile and correct. Their adoption often dictates the choice of follow-up techniques such that if you have pulled back into a cat stance, you cannot now immediately kick with the rear, weight-bearing foot. They tend to present the opponent with a small target profile to aim at whilst allowing you to mobilize all your body weapons without delay. It is unlikely that anyone would face the opponent square-on in horse stance, though they might well be inclined to turn sideways-on. The opponent now has a very limited choice of targets to aim for but, unfortunately, your choice of body weapons is limited to a backfist, or a side-thrust kick.

Use stance to position yourself so all your body weapons are available whilst those of the opponent are inhibited. Thus, if the

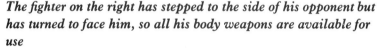

The fighter on the right has stepped to the side of his opponent but has turned to face him, so all his body weapons are available for use

opponent stands with his left foot and left hand leading, then you should move imperceptibly until your leading left foot is in line with his. Then turn your body so your centre-line is directed towards him. If you succeed in doing this without him noticing, then you will be able to attack him directly and with power, whilst he is forced either to rely upon local power, or to turn and face you.

It is not enough to take up and hold a particular stance because any engagement will involve both parties changing range and angle to each other; each seeking a better position from which to launch an attack. Use stances to make a gradual or sudden change in distance and orientation. Therefore be able to draw back, step back, step to either side, step on any one of the four diagonals, or advance into the opponent. Whichever you choose, it is imperative that the stances you adopt are appropriate. It is not sufficient to move in one direction or another; you must move by the right amount, placing the opponent at a disadvantage but remaining able to close distance quickly in order to strike him.

The final consideration is when to move. Even if you move in the required direction by the correct amount, all will avail nothing if you move too quickly, so the opponent notices your intention and redirects his attack. Even worse, moving too slowly in the correct direction may result in the opponent's attack striking home before you have a chance to avoid it. When is the best time to counter his attack? Is it better to attack him even as he attacks you? Or should you withdraw from his attack, let it pass and then attack even as he retrieves it? Both of these are valid strategies. Having said that, some prefer the latter method whilst others, such as Mantis Boxers, go forward to engage the opponent.

Movements

Having taken all these points on board, it is now necessary to look at three methods of stepping used in Shaolin systems. The first is sometimes called *arrow walking*. This is very common and is used in both advancing and retreating modes. Begin from a stance which has one leg leading the other. Slide the front foot forward by about half a pace. Too much of a step warns the opponent, so step by a small amount only. Slide the rear foot up and the original stance length will be reconstituted. Repeat this movement as you close engagement distance with the opponent but check that your stance remains of constant length. Also practise arrow walking as you pull back from the opponent.

Slide forward on the front foot and draw the rear foot up behind it, so you move forward into the opponent

The next form of movement between stances is called *semi-circular stepping*. The rear foot sweeps forward and in, so it passes close to the ankle of the leading foot. Then it sweeps out again to set up a stance similar to the one you began from. This is slower than a direct step but it confuses the opponent and allows you to quickly change orientation and line. Watch out for attacks as your foot is sweeping inwards. Practise stepping back from attacks, using the semicircular movement to take you back and out of the direct thrust.

Slide forward on your front foot

Bring your rear foot forward and in

Continue the u-step, so your moving foot glides past the supporting leg and then continues in an outwards direction. Change your guard at this time

Advancing semicircular stepping combines the two previous forms in that it involves both a direct step with the leading foot followed by a semicircular step with the back foot. The initial sliding step can be in any direction and the following step allows you to turn your body to any angle. This is the most advanced and elegant form of Shaolin stepping movements and it deserves a great deal of attention. It should also be practised whilst moving backwards.

Step directly forward and punch, using momentum of the moving body to increase impact energy

Opposite top: Scissors stepping behind the supporting foot sets the hips up for a side-thrust kick

Opposite bottom: The Mantis boxer attacks the opponent's shin, drawing back into cat stance and striking downwards with his fist

Direct stepping techniques are also encountered in the Shaolin systems. A typical one might be stepping forward with the rear foot whilst holding the guard stationary. Just as weight descends on the stepping foot, so the leading guard hand delivers a vertical punch. This is effective because the step moves the centre of gravity forward behind the punch, thereby adding weight to it.

Horse stance presents a few problems in terms of mobility because it requires a *scissors step* to advance or withdraw. The scissors step takes the rear leg forward in front of or behind the leading foot. The choice between these two will depend upon the following-up techniques to be used. Stepping behind the supporting foot turns the hips away from the target and makes it easy to perform a side-thrust kick. Stepping in front of the supporting leg

leaves the hips and shoulders unchanged, so a backfist can be used without delay. Length of the scissors step is adapted to suit the distance to be closed.

Sometimes it is enough merely to withdraw in a normal stance by sliding the foot back. The body's centre of gravity is brought back over the rear foot, so weight comes off the leading foot. Thus when an attacking front kick falls short, the Mantis boxer is able to attack the shin with a powerful punch.

When is it correct to move? This is a critical question, and various answers are offered. One is that you should study the opponent's eyes because the onset of any powerful technique is seen there first in the form of a narrowing. However, there may be some problems when the opponent already has slitted eyes, or his eyes are not easily visible (e.g., it is dark). Counting against this suggestion is the thought that looking into the eyes of a relentless and skilful opponent is likely to prove dispiriting. A third criticism of the eye-narrowing answer is that no one has yet been struck by an opponent's eyes!

The traditional Shaolin approach is to consider the head and shoulders of the opponent in the form of a triangle with the head at the vertex. Here, an obvious movement can be detected before it gets under way and a response made.

If the first part of effective movement is early recognition of a cue, the next part must be generation of an appropriate technique. It is no use lowering the head to avoid a punch, and moving directly into the path of a knee strike. Once the cue has been picked out and recognised, the body should be capable of responding without conscious thought. And this is what Shaolin training aimed at. If the same sequence of techniques are practised over and over again, they become what is known as 'grooved-in'. This means that they will be evoked automatically each time the appropriate stimulus is made.

Think of this in the same way as an automatic reflex action. You inadvertently touch a hot surface and the hand is snapped away without conscious thought. There is no time to think 'my hand is burning, I must move'. The response is so quick that it happens virtually before the higher brain centres register the sensation of pain. Now it may not be possible to groove-in techniques to the same extent as these automatic reactions (there will always be at least a semi-conscious need to choose between two or more appropriate techniques) but the degree of processing will be reduced to the stage where a really fast response is feasible.

7 Shaolin Body Weapons

The human body is the same now as it was at the foundation of Shaolin Temple. Thus it is fair to claim that there are no new body weapons to be discovered which have not already been used and reused over the centuries. Therefore we can confidently extrapolate back from today's martial art practice and say that the following weapons must have been used, to a greater or lesser extent, in Shaolin Temple.

The Fist

The first of these is obviously the fist. It is capable of being accelerated to a high speed and possesses enough mass to inflict injury. However, the knuckle bones are covered by only a thin layer of skin, so injuries are all too easy to sustain. Thus a degree of toughening-up is required. Secondly, the wrist joint is apt to flex and sprain if it is unprepared for impact. This can happen when the opponent moves suddenly, so the fist strikes the target earlier than expected. The fist must be rolled tightly on itself, so as to exclude air. This gives it a very solid feel. However, take care to ensure that the muscular action needed to close the fist does not extend past the elbow, thereby slowing the punch. Practise rolling the punch tightly, whilst repeatedly flexing and straightening the elbow. The fist must clench sharply if it is to be effective, so training should aim to produce a rapid and intense contraction the instant the knuckles first contact the target. This will enable you to close the fist and make safe contact, even if it is interrupted on its way to the target.

Since the fist is rounded, it follows that not all of the knuckles can make contact with the target. Accordingly different styles tend to use different parts of the fist. Thus, long-hand boxing styles tend to use the knuckles of the index and middle fingers. This is quite a small contact area, so it is effective at transmitting force.

The fist is the most frequently used of all the Shaolin hand weapons

These two knuckles are sometimes associated with a corkscrew action of the forearm that rotates the fist from a palm-upwards to a palm-downwards position on impact. Short-hand boxing styles tend to use the lower three knuckles in what is sometimes known as the vertical fist configuration; i.e., with the thumb uppermost.

Extending the index middle joint forward produces *one-knuckle fist*, a common technique in nearly all of the Shaolin systems. The index finger is locked out by squeezing the thumb tightly against it. This is a very effective way of localizing power into a very small area with the result that blows cause extreme pain and the likelihood of injuring the opponent is much increased. So effective is this technique that some styles – such as Praying Mantis – use it more frequently even than the regular fist.

However, even as the single knuckle is effective at channelling force, so it is susceptible to injury when used indiscriminately. It

*Extending the index knuckle forward produces what is called
'one knuckle fist'. Use this to attack targets such as the
opponent's temples*

therefore follows that a certain amount of conditioning is essential
to get the best from it. One-knuckle fist is used to attack virtually
every target available to regular front fist, though novices are
advised to concentrate on using it against such targets as the ribs,
solar plexus, base of breastbone, and angle of jaw and temple.

Backfist is common to all styles of boxing and is either delivered
with a nearly straight, rapidly swinging arm, or by sudden elbow
extension. The former produces a 'haymaker' action that is both
powerful and easily seen (if not easily avoided). The latter is much
shorter, snappier but rather less powerful. Note that power may be
generated either by turning the body into the strike, or unrolling
the shoulders away from the punching action. The second method
produces a faster, longer range punch but the first method is more
powerful. Both elbow powered versions of backfist rely upon the
joint's natural elasticity to provide quick retrieval.

Use vertical backfist to attack the bridge of the opponent's nose

Backfist can be applied vertically to targets such as the bridge of the nose, or horizontally to the temples or side of jaw. As with the front punch, the fist contracts tightly on first contact but then immediately relaxes. Some styles use a whiplash action of the wrist for extra speed.

Hammerfist uses the cushioned area of muscle immediately below the little finger, making it unlikely to suffer injury through accidental collision with a bony surface. Strikes are made in the manner of hammering an imaginary nail into the opponent. They can be delivered horizontally into the spine, kidneys, ribs, solar plexus, temple or jaw, or vertically onto the top of the head or the collar bones. Bending the knees on impact adds bodyweight and produces a very powerful action indeed. A backwards upswinging strike can be used against the groin or chin.

Opening the fist half-way produces a little-used technique that is

84

Horizontal backfist can be used against any target on the side of the opponent's body or head. The jaw is an obvious target to aim for

used to attack the throat. It slips in easily below the jaw, where there is insufficient clearance for an orthodox front fist. *Half-open fist* is also used horizontally to attack the ribs, or vertically to attack the base of the breast bone. However, half-open fist is not a strong configuration because, not only is the wrist liable to flex on impact, but the finger joints are too. This is therefore a low-energy weapon. Even were it not so, it would prove difficult to toughen the middle knuckles sufficiently to withstand hard impact against a bony target.

Above: Use descending hammerfist to attack the back of the opponent's head. Bending the knees adds extra force to the impact

Right: Use hammerfist also for a backwards-travelling strike into the opponent's groin

Other Uses of the Hand

Extending the fingers of half-open fist produces what we may refer to as *claw hand*, though it goes by a number of different titles (e.g. bear claw) in the different schools. This is a dangerous hand weapon used to great effect against the face, where the hooked fingers catch in the various hollows and can cause disfiguring injuries. Exponents of claw hand train to such an extent that the weapon becomes extremely powerful and the fingers are able to fasten onto what they catch and tear it. It is a low-energy weapon insofar as it does not need to be thrown at great speed into the target to achieve its effect. Instead, it is an active weapon, producing its effects once it has found the target.

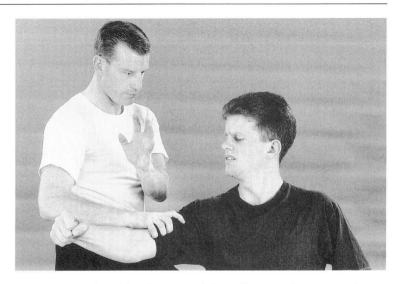

Above: Claw hand is what we might call 'an active weapon'. Experienced Shaolin martial artists were able to inflict severe pain by sinking the fingertips into the opponent's flesh

Opposite top: Palm-heel uses the pad of flesh at the base of the palm to attack targets such as the chin. Use either a straight, jolting movement . . .

Opposite bottom: . . . or a curving strike that sharply twists the opponent's head, producing an effective knock-out

Use claw hand in a downwards-striking arc to the face, an upwards-travelling movement into the groin, or a simple grasping attack to the opponent's limbs. Its application is often said to simulate that of a leopard or tiger.

Extending the fingers fully produces a very common short-hand weapon known as the *palm-heel*. Like hammerfist, this is effective because the relevant bones are cushioned by a pad of muscle. Furthermore, there are no joints to flex under a hard impact so the technique is both safe and rigid. Palm-heels are used in a variety of ways, the most simple being in the form of a straight thrust to the chin, kidneys, or base of the breast bone. Curving thrusts glance the palm-heel across the side of the jaw, producing a turning action that is very effective at causing a knock-out. Short-range thrusts bring the elbows close to the body, so the strike travels near vertically into the opponent's chin.

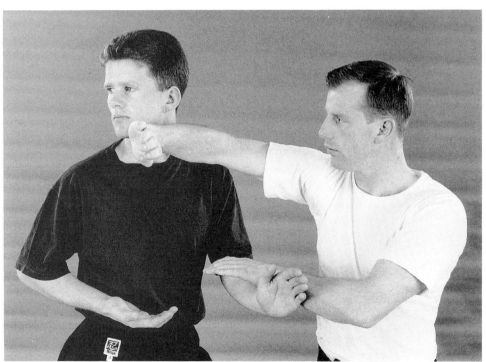

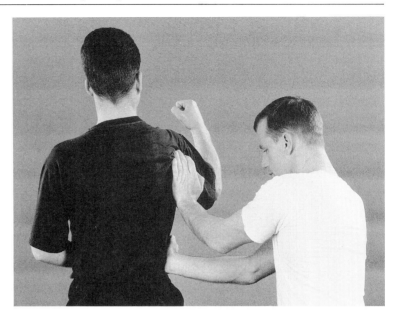

Butterfly hand uses a double palm-heel to attack targets such as the shoulderblades/kidneys

A characteristic of Shaolin systems is the double palm-heel, sometimes known as *butterfly hand*. This has the fingers of the upper hand pointing upwards whilst those of the lower point downwards. Typically this strike is applied to the opponent's chest and ribs, or to his shoulderblades and kidneys. Sometimes a double palm-heel (but not butterfly hand) is used in an upwards travelling strike to the opponent's jaw. A cupped palm-heel also forms the basis of a number of blocks.

Tilting the wrist forwards produces two varieties of weapon, the *spear hand* and the *knife hand*. Taking the former first , spear hand is one of those weapons which are all but unusable without proper conditioning. This is because the middle finger tends to buckle on impact unless drawn back to the same length as the index and third finger. Even when the fingers are drawn back into one line, spearhand continues to be prone to flexing. For this reason, it is generally placed with other low-energy weapons and is only used against the opponent's vital areas. But this is only half its potential use. With proper training, spear hand is a very effective weapon for attacking the sternum, throat and ribs. The hand orientation changes from thumb-upwards to palm-downwards, according to its application.

90

Above: A cupped palm-heel is used as an effective block
*Below: Spear hand needs a great deal of conditioning before it
can be used effectively as a weapon*

91

Knife hand is often referred to as a 'chop' and this eloquently describes how it is applied. The fingers are slightly cupped and the thumb is tucked inwards. Knife strike travels in an arc, with the hand tightening up on impact, much like the front fist. The most powerful knife hand strikes rotate the forearm just before impact, so the hand turns either palm upwards-facing, or downwards-facing. Knife hand can be applied in a forehand, back hand, vertical or horizontal manner but perhaps the most often used version is the horizontal forehand strike into the side of the opponent's neck or jaw. This makes use of a wide swinging action in which both shoulders play a part in generating energy. A backwards-travelling knife hand can be used against an opponent standing to the side. Use it to attack the throat or bridge of nose.

A vertical knife hand strikes down onto the collarbones and is made even stronger by flexing the knees slightly on impact. Also use it to strike backwards and up into the opponent's groin.

Knife hand can be used in the reverse direction, when impact is made with the thumb-edge of the hand. This is used following a sideways evasion of the opponent's advance. Swing it around and

The most commonly used knife hand strike employs a forehand motion, delivering the side of the slightly cupped palm into the side of the opponent's neck or jaw

Top: A backwards-travelling knife hand strike is useful when you are not facing the opponent

Above: A vertical knife hand can be used to attack the collarbones. Bend your knees slightly as the strike is about to hit the target

into the opponent's throat, or bring it up sharply into his groin.

Bent wrist is sometimes used as a strike, though it is more commonly used as a rising block against the opponent's punch. The fingers and thumb are brought together to form a beak-like weapon that is used to attack the opponent's face or collarbones.

Forearms and Elbows

The forearms too are used as weapons, but in the sense of a crushing block that damages the opponent's elbow. *Elbow strike* is an essential part of the syllabus of nearly all the Shaolin systems and it is used in a variety of ways. All involve a swinging action of some form or another – whether horizontal or vertical. The elbow may travel forwards into the target, or backwards into the opponent's face or solar plexus. In all cases, the fist is clenched tightly to protect the elbow joint from injury.

A forward strike on the reverse side to the leading leg is one of the most powerful, wiping the elbow across the opponent's face and jaw. An upwards strike functions like an uppercut, clipping the jaw and knocking the head backwards. A downwards strike descends upon the back of the opponent's bowed head or neck. Note how the knees are suddenly bent to add body weight to the descending weapon. Downwards strike can also be used to good effect against the opponent's collarbones. A backwards-travelling strike into the opponent's face or sternum is effective when you are standing sideways-on.

Kicks

Kicks, especially those using the ball of the foot, are more in evidence in those Shaolin styles described as 'northern' (*cho chiao* for example), where engagement distances are such as to require a step forward before a punch can be used. An exception to this is the *knee attack*. However it is fair to set this apart as a special case because it is a short-range leg technique that can be used inside punching range – provided that the opponent has first been diverted. Without this diversion, a knee attack can easily result in you being unceremoniously dumped onto your back!

Thrusting kicks use the heel of the foot (and so are also known as heel kicks), with the toes angled to either side. The heel is a tough weapon, already hardened through bearing the body's weight, so it needs no conditioning. The outer edge of the foot is a subsidiary

94

Top: A forwards elbow strike wipes the elbow across the side of the opponent's jaw

Above: An upwards-travelling elbow strike functions just like an uppercut

Top: Descending elbow strike is typically used to attack the back of the opponent's head. Flex your knees slightly to increase the force of impact

Above: Use backwards-travelling elbow strike against an opponent standing immediately behind you

Opposite top: Thrusting kicks use the heel of the foot to attack the target – in this case the opponent's groin

Opposite bottom: Sometimes the foot is twisted, so the little toe-edge functions as a subsidiary impact area

97

weapon, rather than a weapon in itself. It is used more in the northern styles with a sharp, snapping action rather than a powerful thrust. The inside edge of the foot is sometimes used to scoop the opponent's guard to one side, though it can also be applied to the side of the opponent's face. The instep is used against the opponent's groin in a fast snapping action that drops the spent foot in exactly the right position to deliver a series of follow-up punches and strikes.

Other kicks include: back kick, axe kick, butterfly kick, crescent kick, front kick, front-leg kick, side kick and stamping kick.

Conditioning and Training

It is now time to consider the matter of body toughening and the comments made here apply primarily to hand-conditioning. Most people would agree that it is no use developing a great deal of impact power if the weapons used to apply it are weak. It may be possible to develop enough power to break a brick but what is the use of that if every time you do so, you break a bone? It is therefore essential to develop the hands into effective weapons. This will inspire confidence in your ability to hurt the opponent because whilst the opponent's punch may be dangerous, you know that yours is equally, if not more so.

Condition your hands until the knuckles become like a series of equally raised iron-hard marbles with the natural gaps between them all but filled out. Only then will the energy being developed prove effective. Achieve this goal by punching wall-bags filled with varying mixtures of beans and sand. This causes redness and soreness but continue anyway! Rub embrocation into the knuckles after training and this will keep the skin smooth and unscarred. But beware of training in such a way that the knuckles become scarred and obviously disfigured.

Once you have progressed to training against bags filled with sand, change to a bag containing small ball-bearings. This still gives slightly under impact and finishes off fist-conditioning. Perfectionists may wish to go to still greater lengths by punching wall-bags containing iron-dust or shingle!

However, note that over-toughening the fist can lead to fatigue fractures. Avoid this by easing back when the knuckles become bruised. Whenever the filling in the bag is changed for a harder composition, the knuckles will become sore all over again. Remain

Condition your fists by punching wall-bags filled with a mixture of beans and sand

with that particular filling until the soreness abates before changing to a still harder mix. But whichever mix you use, don't forget to use embrocation after each training session and if you can't get hold of the traditional Chinese ointment, then use any proprietary brand. A proper application reduces inflammation and soreness of the joints and muscles.

Avoid poor technique in which the fist lands on one knuckle all the time. This leads to an unequal enlargement of the knuckle bones and makes it difficult to condition the whole fist.

Train for spear hand by thrusting the fingers against wall-bags containing different mixes of beans and sand. Then go on to striking against cardboard boxes. The traditional method was to thrust the fingers between bundles of rice straw bound tightly at top and bottom. When the monk could do this, the straw was changed for slivers of bamboo.

99

Use wall-bags to toughen knife hand. Strike hard – as though you were actually trying to penetrate the bag

Use wall-bags to toughen knife hand and to penetrate the training-bag – don't be content just to rain heavy blows on its surface.

Claw hand can be toughened in a number of ways. The first and most traditional was for pairs of monks to throw a heavy piece of rough stone to each other and snatch it out of the air with downward swipes of claw hand. Some masters drove their hands into mixtures of sand and flour until they were tough enough to be plunged into bowls filled with pebbles. The final stage of this training (known as *kan shu*) was thrusting the hands into a bucketful of stones heated over a brazier!

Forearms are trained by pairs of students banging them together in a series of striking and blocking actions. Sometimes a wooden dummy was used instead of a partner. This consisted of a vertical baulk of timber representing the body, with short spars to

100

Shaolin martial artists toughened their forearms by striking them against their partner's

represent the arms and legs. These were sunk into the ground to give them rigidity and Shaolin students had to 'fight' with a series of such dummies, practising a different sequence of attacks and defences on each.

However, it is not enough merely to toughen the weapons. It is inevitable that you will receive the odd blow during training, so it is essential that you toughen your body too. The best way to achieve this is to spar without protection, contracting the muscles of the stomach each time a blow is expected. For most of us, adequate body conditioning occurs naturally through training, though this does require that the partner be allowed to regularly land hard blows during practice.

Vital Points

The next thing to consider is the body's so called 'vital points'. The concept of vital areas is common to both martial art and Chinese medicine, and involves identifying channels of living energy flowing through the human body. The vital points of the body are said to be those where the body's energy channels (*ching lo*) are susceptible to a second party's intervention. Whether this intervention arises from the healing hands of a physician, or through a blow from the skilled martial artist makes no difference insofar as the flow of energy along a particular pathway is stimulated or inhibited. The physician will try to encourage energy to flow along a channel, or 'meridian', in order to balance the body. A martial-art expert intent on causing mayhem will stop energy flow, causing imbalance, injury and in some cases, eventual death.

The extent to which such vital points were used, or even known of by the monks of Shaolin is a matter for conjecture. However, the practice of attacking the body's vital points (*dim mok*) is well known and it is unlikely that it escaped the attention of the temple during its long martial history.

The body's principal energy centre (*dan tien*) is said to lie in the area of the navel. Chinese traditionalists actually distinguish three centres here, in a vertical sequence. They function like cisterns, so that as the lowest fills, its energy spills over into the next. And so on. When energy is produced in the body, it circulates from the mid-section along meridian channels, travelling both upwards towards the head and downwards to the feet. From there it returns to collecting centres, for eventual return to the main energy centres. In the event that energy production is low, the meridians conduct nothing and the person feels depleted and fatigued. If the energy is interrupted, then the imbalance mentioned above occurs and symptoms of illness appear.

There is a point on the sole of the foot where energy travels upwards to the energy centres. This is stimulated in the Chinese healing art of reflexology. There is a second energy centre in the middle of the palm from which energy can be directed outwards and into the body of another person. However, unlike the centre for energy production in the abdomen, these two points are simply

The practice of attacking the body's vital points is well known to Chinese martial artists

102

gates through which energy can flow. A third and very important energy conduit lies on the back, near the kidneys. This area is extremely vulnerable to hard blows which, in consequence, have a very damaging effect upon the health! There is a fourth energy gate on the crown of the head that corresponds with one of the fontanelles of the infant's skull.

A hard blow into the body's main energy centre produces an immediate effect upon the diaphragm, so breathing is impaired. When this happens, tranquillity is lost and the person becomes subject to fear or anxiety. Even more serious is a longer-term adverse effect upon major organs such as the liver, spleen, stomach and gall bladder.

The body's vital areas often appear to be related to nerve ganglia and blood vessels. So though we might dismiss the notion of an impalpable energy field, we can nevertheless see how stimulation of these various areas might produce an effect. The picture becomes even more sophisticated when one considers that the Chinese physician or martial artist is able to elicit effects in one part of the body by stimulating an apparently unrelated part. How is this so? During the development of a human embryo, the various parts are separated into primordial segments known as somites. These somites become widely separated in the adult, yet they retain a link. Thus it is that if your spleen is damaged, you often feel a pain at the tip of your left shoulder!

So it is evident that there is more to the Chinese notion of vital areas than mere superstition. In fact the notion has arisen out of hundreds of years of patient enquiry and analysis. So though we may nowadays dispute the theory, the practical observations remain worthy of consideration. Particularly interesting are the discoveries of the physiologist Jean-Paul Allard. He has convincingly shown that stimulation of many of the vital areas by a blow of some sort does have a measurable effect upon the individual concerned. In some cases, he has identified areas which, if struck with accuracy and force, might well cause the death of the victim!

8 Shaolin Blocking Techniques

It is possible to take what is called a backbearing from the most common blocks found in many present-day Shaolin systems to what plainly were core blocking techniques used in the temple at various stages in its long history. Indeed, the modern Shaolin blocking systems are by far the most sophisticated of any far-eastern martial art and it is instructive to examine the ways in which each of the core blocks described here has been subsequently modified by the various schools. First of all, we will spend some time on identifying the crucial elements required for an effective block. Then we will see how the Shaolin blocks were developed to take these points on board.

Fundamentals

The first and most obvious point about blocking is that it must be done quickly enough to cope with a fast attack. This rules out any extraneous and unnecessary actions, such as the so called 'pulley – principle blocks' which rely upon the pull-back of the non-blocking arm to generate power for the blocking action. It also rules against circular blocks, though with the proviso that such blocks may be the most effective for less-skilled students to use. The rule is therefore that blocking actions should use only the minimum of movement to produce the desired effect. Only then can they be employed quickly enough. In practical terms, this reduces all blocks to a short, crisp action in which deflection is achieved not by force, but by correct application.

Secondly, blocks must aim for maximum efficiency of deflection of the incoming technique. Novices often fail to achieve this, so a punch aimed at the jaw is swept upwards by a rising block, into the forehead. Poor mid-section blocks deflect attacks aimed at the solar plexus into the ribs and ineffective lower blocks sweep a kick into the hip. The converse situation is also to be avoided, i.e., where the attack is deflected well to the side. This is wasteful because it then takes longer to retrieve the blocking arm. The second rule of good blocking is therefore that deflection must be adequate, but not excessive. The old saying 'a miss is as good as a mile' applies here.

The third point is the specificity of blocks. Many blocks are fairly specialized or restricted in their application and, when misapplied, the attacking technique is not deflected. Specialized blocks are typically used by skilled martial artists who are able to correctly interpret the cues that tell them which attacking technique is on its way. Such specialized blocks often use only a small part of the body – such as the palm of the hand – to sweep the attack in the correct direction. But the palm of the hand has a small deflection surface cross-section, and if you are inaccurate when using it . . . Contrast this with forearm blocks. These use the whole length of the forearm, giving a sweep of up to 30 centimetres in height. Clearly this provides a much wider margin of error. Double blocks increase this margin still further. The rule, then, is: use the correct block for the technique. More skilled students should use specific blocks; less skilled students should use general or double blocks.

The fourth point is that the blocking action must be applied correctly to the attacking technique. Blocks are usually active rather than passive. This is to say that they apply controlled force to deflect the attacker's energy. Contrast this with passive blocking, where a limb is simply left in the path of the attack. Though deflection energies need not be great to achieve an effect, they nevertheless must be applied in the correct manner. Thus, a lower block must not meet a kick at a 90 degrees collision angle because, if it does, the forearm and wrist are virtually guaranteed to lose their battle against the shin.

Still on this fourth point, note that the blocking action can be made more active by rotating the forearm. This stiffens the arm, makes the elbow joint more resilient and adds an extra sharpness to the blocking impact.

Top: The person on the right has blocked to the wrong side of his opponent's punch

Bottom: This encourages the opponent to use his other fist in a follow-up attack

Block the person, not his technique. Here the block has passed through the opponent's leading hand, barring it against his own body, and gone through to strike him

The fifth point about Shaolin blocks is that they were not aimed solely at the attacking technique itself. Consider a basic forearm block which sweeps an incoming punch to the side. If you block on the wrong side, you merely turn the opponent's upper body and encourage him to use his other fist. Even if you block him on his closed side, he can still withdraw and counterattack. You must therefore block into him, cutting through his technique as you do so. Your block must travel outwards from your body and into the opponent. Never block with a sweep that travels simply from low to high, or from side to side. Rather use an action which travels diagonally.

There is a second benefit to doing this. The incoming technique requires time to develop full power and going out to meet it means deflecting it before that full power is developed. Furthermore, blocking well out from your body provides a margin of error in

108

Turn your centre-line towards the opponent as you block. This is vital if you want to develop an effective counter

which to do something, should the block fail. However, it is not clever to advance into the opponent with your chin as you apply the block! Keep your back near to vertical, though a slight forward lean is permissible. Relax your shoulders, letting them curve forward and keep control of your arms. Novices concentrate on the blocking action and ignore what the other hand is doing. Shaolin blocks use both arms together in an economical way, never moving either more than is strictly necessary.

The sixth point is about always keeping your body turned so your centre-line faces the opponent. This is a classic Shaolin rule. Therefore each time you block, go into the opponent, projecting your blocking energy through your own centre-line. Do not turn your body away from the attack because although this may well cause it to miss, it also prevents you from responding effectively. Turn your body even as the opponent does, so you are always

109

110

Above: Block in such a way that at least one hand is near the opponent's target areas. In this case, the right hand is ideally placed for a following palm-heel strike

Opposite top: Turning your body away may well assist your block but it slows your follow-up . . .

Opposite bottom: . . . so the opponent may get there first!

facing him squarely. Use the principle of line to stand in front and slightly to one side of him, so whilst you are facing him directly, he is slightly turned from you. Only an imperceptible sideways movement need be made. Indeed, step too much and he will see what you are doing and turn to face you. The maxim to adopt is: always keep your body directly facing his.

The seventh point concerns the position of your hands as you block and it begins where an earlier comment left off. Block in such a manner that at least one of your hands is near the target. Only then can a counterattack be applied quickly enough. Beware

111

Advanced Shaolin blocks use the same action to both block . . .

of blocking the opponent and then having to retrieve your non-blocking arm from the hip. Bring both fists close to the opponent so you can strike him quickly with either. The most advanced Shaolin blocks combine deflection with a counterattack, so the opponent's punch is first deflected, then the deflecting hand carries on into the opponent's face. Such techniques, however, require a formidable level of skill.

The eighth point reiterates and adds to one we looked at a moment ago. Do not let your block cross your own centre-line. Not only is this unnecessary, it also makes the technique weak. Keep each hand to its respective side of the body and you will be able to use it directly. Lose control of your hands so they cross the centre-line willy-nilly and you will first have to retrieve them before you can apply a powerful technique. Use body evasion to set you up in the correct position for any block. Don't just flail your arms about and expect them to stop a determined attack.

112

. . . and attack

Remember, a block does not just entail moving your arms; you must position your body too.

The ninth point concerns the application of power during the blocking action. Typically novices 'focus' their blocks and go for maximum power at the end of the movement. This is not a wise thing to do because the attack may contact your block before the latter is ready for it. The block then fails and injury is likely. The converse tactic, trying to block with a rigid arm, does not work either because taut muscles reduce limb speed. Aim to make the block effective throughout its range of movement, so even if you are caught unprepared, you aren't left defenceless. The answer is to use whole-body energy and to move into the attack. Many Shaolin systems do not advocate stepping back from an attack because a skilled opponent will then simply move forward and force you further onto the defensive.

Head block uses an upward-rolling action of the blocking forearm, which catches the opponent high on his attacking arm

Specific Blocks

There are at least four types of head block, of which the *upwards rolling block* is perhaps the most interesting. As its name implies, this version uses a rising and rolling action of the blocking forearm to deflect the opponent's punch upwards. However, it is not enough simply to bump the fist upwards; the forearm must rotate as it rises, so the little-finger edge finishes uppermost. Ensure that the degree of deflection is adequate, so the punch clears the head and the blocking forearm does not obscure the eyes.

The skilled user turns his body into the attacker, so the centreline is directed towards the opponent. The blocking forearm rises and rotates in the normal manner but a shrugging action of the shoulders takes it forwards as well as up, changing it into an upwards *diagonal* movement that closes with the attacking technique. Sometimes this means that the block is applied high on the

114

Turn your body into the opponent, so you thrust his attack away and close him off. Notice how you can attack with your left fist but the opponent can use nothing at all

opponent's arm, though this need not always be the case.

Do not lean forward as you apply the block. This is a common fault which shows an incorrect usage of power. It is also dangerous because it brings the face too close to the opponent. Use only the power of your shoulder and the springiness of your elbow to make the block effective. Don't make the mistake of locking up the rest of the body because if you do, an immediate follow-up is made impossible. If you find yourself too far away to block correctly, then use a short forward slide or arrow step to close distance and, if necessary, adjust your angle by means of a turning motion of the body.

It is true that you can now punch under the blocked arm except that the opponent also has a fist which is cocked and ready for use. It is therefore better to close the opponent off, preventing him from using his other arm by following with a *hooking forearm block*.

115

This forces the opponent's trapped arm across his upper body, so obscuring his counter attack.

Inner forearm block uses a rotational forearm action coupled with a windscreen wiper-like action of the shoulder joint to swing the forearm up and into the opponent's punching arm. The elbow is bent so the blocking hand – usually a fist – is level with the top of your shoulder. Note that it is very dangerous to over-straighten the arm since this makes the block very weak. This is why the novice is always taught to keep his elbow close to the ribs. Turn into the direction of the block as it is being applied. This generates power from the hip. Then thrust both shoulders forward in a shrugging action similar to that used in the head block described above. The forearm travels diagonally forward and across the body (though it never crosses the centre-line!) with the thumb uppermost. Then the hip engages and the hand rotates to a palm-upwards position. The block no longer therefore simply strikes the attacking limb; instead it travels forward and into the opponent. This sometimes means that the opponent is blocked higher up his arm.

Step forward to close distance and never lean forward since this advances the chin. Provided you thrust hard enough forwards with the block, it is not even necessary to rotate the hand fully, and satisfactory blocks can be made with the thumb upwards. Remember: do not block against the attack, block forward and into it! From a tactical point of view, a correctly applied inner forearm block not only deflects an attack, it also opens the opponent up to your counterattack.

Though your elbow will straighten further in advanced versions of this block, you must not extend the arm fully. A straight arm is weak and vulnerable, whereas a slightly flexed elbow is resilient and powerful. Strengthen the elbow by clenching the fingers and stiffening the wrist slightly. Do not allow your elbow to swing outwards since this also weakens the blocking action.

Novices practise *outer block* with a chopping action, using the little finger edge of the hand and side of the wrist and forearm to knock an attack to the side. The blocking action is enhanced by both a hip twist and a wide circular action that sweeps the forearm across the body. Ignore the idea of pulling back the non-blocking arm even in elementary practice, since this is both slow and wasteful of effort. The *advanced outer block* uses much the same action except that the block changes from chopping, to thrusting hand. Impact is on the forearm and back of wrist, with the palm turned upwards.

Inner forearm block travels forward as it curves outwards. Note how the block has closed the opponent off and the right hand is near his face for an immediate follow-up

Take up stance and turn your hips away from the direction in which you will block. Extend your right arm and fingers, turning the hand palm-downwards. Fold the left forearm across your body. Twist your hips strongly to face the opponent and, as the shoulders turn to their new position, fold your extended right arm so the elbow moves into the ribs. Begin rotating the right hand even as it thrusts out; don't leave the final twist until the last moment. Tighten the muscle of the forearm and wrist sharply as the palm turns upwards.

The kinetics of outer block are very important. There must be a slight delay between the hips turning and the shoulders following. This builds up a twisting tension in the spinal muscles, pre-loading them with power. Allow a further slight delay between the shoulders turning to their final position and the extension of the blocking arm. This stretches and preloads the lateral and pectoral

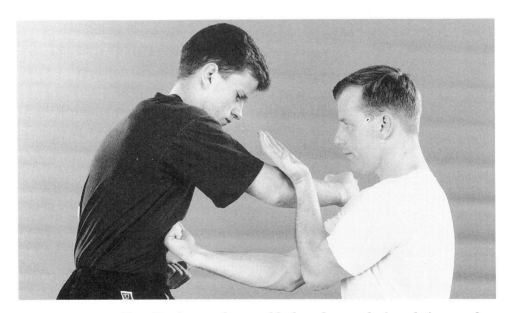

Top: Novices apply outer block to the attacker's technique, rather than to the attacker himself

Above: Then the other hand is used to attack the floating ribs

118

Advanced outer block thrusts into the opponent, deflecting his technique on the way and leaving your blocking hand close enough to attack immediately

muscles so the final thrusting action is made even stronger. Finally, shrug your shoulders forward and lead with the blocking shoulder.

Each part of the movement must flow smoothly into the next at just the right time. Avoid jerkiness and accelerate smoothly all the way to the final position. By these means, the block becomes a thrust into the opponent's body which, on the way, encounters and deflects his punch.

Another type of Shaolin forearm block uses neither the inside nor the outside of the forearm – it uses the lower surface. Because the wrist is generally bent forwards as the technique is applied, I have described this deflection as *hooking forearm block*. Hooking block is quite a strong technique because it is thrust forwards and into the opponent with a palm-downwards hand position. This allows the lower forearm to glance over the top of the attacking technique and strike into the opponent's face.

As with outer block, the kinetics of hooking block are all-

119

important. Deliver it with a twisting motion of the hips that turns the blocking side towards the opponent. Follow with a shrugging action of the shoulders, thrusting your blocking arm forward and into the opponent's punch or grab. Step forward to close distance, barring the opponent's blocked arm across his own body. He will find it impossible to push your arm away because he is pushing against your body, not just against your arm.

The palm of the hand makes an effective, fast *slapping block* which can be used either horizontally or vertically. It smacks the incoming technique off-course, striking near the wrist or ankle, where great leverage is not necessary. Slapping block is interesting in that, alone of all the Shaolin blocks, it can cross the centre-line of your body with impunity. This is because the action is so fast and the block is withdrawn so quickly that the opponent has no chance to exploit its weakness. A second point of interest is that it tends to be used more from a distance, so you are then obliged to step forward to reach the opponent with your counterattack. This is why slapping block is so often combined with a kick.

The hand must be configured correctly for slapping block, such

120

Left: Hooking forearm block is particularly strong and bars the opponent's arm across his body

Above: Palm block can be used vertically downwards . . .

121

. . . vertically upwards (left) . . .

. . . or (above) as a horizontal technique that bars the opponent's arm across his own body

that the palm is slightly cupped. This stiffens the forearm and makes the wrist more resilient. The fingers remain straight and tight together whilst the thumb curls around to reinforce the palm. The incoming technique is caught by what almost amounts to a cupped palm.

Slapping block is applied exactly like hooking block, so the novice's simple slap changes to a strong thrust into the opponent. This causes the block to strike higher up the opponent's arm, closing his body off and preventing a fast follow up. Power comes from a twisting motion of the hips combined with a shrugging action of the shoulders. The blocking shoulder leads, though the face should not be brought forward.

Top: Circling hand is not a block at all. Here your wrist has been seized by the opponent

Above: Circle your wrist, forcing the little finger-edge of your palm against the opponent's wrist. Withdraw your arm as you do this

Circling hand is not really a block as such, though I have included it here for convenience. It is used to break free from the opponent's grasp by rotating the hand against his thumb.

Lower block travels in a powerful, shallow downwards arc to sweep a wide area free from attacking techniques. However, the blocking elbow is never fully straightened. It is always slightly bent so the block is strong and resilient. This resilience is helped by a strong hand position in which the fingers are clenched and the wrist bent. The novice is taught to move well away from the attack, perhaps simultaneously using his other arm in an outer block. This sweeps a very wide area indeed and is excellent for making safe.

Lower block slices down in an arc to sweep a wide area of the lower body free of attacking techniques

Use a double block to carry the fight to your opponent. Move into him as he kicks, avoiding his attack by the smallest amount and applying lower block to it

Right: Use double block against fist attacks, where you aren't sure which techniques the opponent is using

126

However, the advanced student will not merely want to make safe but to carry the fight to the opponent. Therefore, *advanced lower block* uses less of a swinging action and more of a downwards thrust. Move diagonally forward so the kick misses by the smallest possible amount. This leaves you close enough to push the opponent completely off balance with a combination of lower block and palm-heel. Use double block also against hand attacks, where you aren't sure what technique the opponent is using.

Scooping block is one of the rare circular Shaolin blocks. It curls the cupped hand under the opponent's kicking heel, lifting it both up and forward. Do not turn your hips away as you block; rather withdraw directly from the kick by rocking back into a short cat stance. Lift the trapped foot and take it to the opponent's closed side, so his centre-line is turned away and his opportunities for immediate counterattack reduced to a wild swinging of his arms.

127

9 Shaolin Fighting Strategy

Sparring

We know that the monks of Shaolin were, at least at different times, formidable fighters. There still remain paintings of the monks engaging in martial-art practice, some of which looks remarkably like sparring. Chinese poets tell us, through their verses, of displays of martial art given by the Shaolin monks. For these to be meaningful to non-martial artists, presumably they must have looked something like fighting and not, perhaps, dancing. From this, we can conclude that some form of sparring took place in the temple. This assertion is strengthened somewhat by accounts of how monks became accepted as teachers, i.e., they were required to fight a number of other teachers. Additionally, certain of the monks became known as famous fighters. How could they have become known as such without having taken part in some form of fighting? So what form did this fighting, or sparring, take?

Firstly we can agree that there is no evidence that Shaolin Temple Boxing was ever practised as a sport. Indeed, one would not expect a religious discipline aimed at removing the ego to encourage an activity which sought to promote it. Even so, one might argue that trying to better one's own mental and physical performance of yesterday constitutes a competitive sport, so a sporting competition need not necessarily be harmful. Further, one could argue that a competition could be understood as a vehicle for defeating one's own ego.

However, one of the problems of practising any kind of martial art as a sport is that of deciding rules. It follows that if the purpose of the martial art is to defeat (often by killing) the opponent by any means available, then, unless rules are instituted, serious injury becomes a real possibility at any competitive event. But, if rules are introduced, then you are no longer competing within a martial art. You may become a good sportsperson but not necessarily an

The wearing of protective equipment during sparring can lead to undesirable modification of tactics and technique. The greatest realism accrues when no such equipment is worn

effective martial artist. In fact it may theoretically be possible to win championships whilst being a poor martial artist!

An examination of modern Shaolin competition shows a deep awareness of this difficulty. Thus, in order to preserve the martial art, protective equipment is minimal and techniques are used with unmitigated force. It certainly seems true that if you wear protective equipment, then you will come to rely on it, so the whole method of fighting changes. Thus, an effective face guard may cause you not to bother taking extra care to protect your face, so your defence becomes lax in a real fighting situation.

This is not to say that defensive armour could not be worn and we have no reason to doubt that vests containing bamboo strips were used to mitigate the effects of heavy body blows. If free sparring did take place at Shaolin, then it was probably much like that which occurs in the Chinese colonies, with not a few injuries, some of which are serious.

What we can say with perhaps greater confidence is that prearranged sparring took place between pairs of individuals and this could be the subject of the wall murals at Shaolin. Both attacker and defender know what techniques are to be used, and in what order. This allows both parties to use the full range of techniques with relative safety, yet it teaches concepts such as distance and timing – both of which are difficult to simulate in pattern practice. In its simplest form, prearranged sparring involves the exchange of two techniques: a single attack and a single response to it. In the more advanced forms, such sparring can involve a whole series of techniques and responses, which, between two supremely skilful opponents, gives the impression of an actual fight.

Prearranged sparring is invaluable when you are trying to build up fast conditioned reflexes, and as the pace of action increases, so you spend less and less time in thinking about which move comes next. The trained body takes over and the mind remains detached and unafraid. Even with all these advantages, prearranged sparring remains just that and if you know what technique is to come next, and that you will most probably not be injured, then a degree of realism is lost.

So, what factors are important in any system of sparring? First of all, a restatement is in order. That is, it does not necessarily follow that if you can fight well in the training hall, you will be able to fight well outside. This is perhaps one of the most serious mistakes made by martial artists in general and leads them into making wholly false claims about their ability at martial art practice. When you spar in your club, do you envisage the possibility that the outcome may be a savage beating or possibly even death? Of course not! Yet is this not precisely the state of affairs that obtains on the battlefield?

During most martial art training, students spar only with other martial artists and then within a rules structure intended to minimize the risk of serious injury. Is it not the case that such students become used to the way clubmates attack and respond?

130

Many forms of martial-art sparring are heavily stylized and have conventions which apply only to that school. Thus, members of a school of long-hand boxing will be used to sparring at a certain engagement distance and may find themselves at a positive disadvantage when facing exponents of the short-hand schools.

Is it likely that Shaolin monks found themselves fighting to the death with brother monks? It is surely more likely that they faced unfamiliar patterns of attack and response, performed with a different purpose in mind – including that of inflicting death or serious injury. It therefore follows that the best system of sparring must involve training with students of other schools. Only then can one learn how they respond.

As an aside, nowadays it is not unknown for masters to send their students to other teachers to learn specific techniques that have been perfected in the others' schools. By this means, a reciprocal exchange takes place and there is set up what we might call a 'technique bank', to which others have access. However, access to this only operates between teachers who are not motivated solely by notions of financial gain, and who hold each other in mutual regard. This is not a new idea and a similar exchange programme is mentioned in several old manuscripts. In them, we learn that boxers travelled between masters in order to pick up new elements of footwork or technique.

Returning to the main theme of this chapter, the presence of malice and the absence of protective rules leads to fear, and fear in turn inhibits those techniques which are performed so expertly in the training hall. Muscles are slowed by fear and strength declines. In fact a great many martial artists become so agitated that they forget about technique and the principles of energy application altogether! Other martial artists become so aggressive that all they want to do is close with the opponent and hurt him. These also forget technique and throw caution to the winds. Consequently they become vulnerable.

This leads on to my second point, and that is: a tranquil mind is the single most important element of sparring. Even if you know only a little technique, a calm mind will ensure that you use it to best effect.

The next most important aspects of sparring are power and stamina. Many martial artists are enthusiastic about free sparring but their muscles and stamina let them down! This may be because the element of skill comes to be uppermost in the student's mind, so the importance of stamina and strength are underplayed. There is no doubt that if you are stronger than the opponent and can maintain an effective attacking pressure over a longer period, then the odds are stacked heavily in your favour. If you can hit someone and injure them, then all other considerations become secondary.

Strength also plays an important role in protecting the internal organs from injury, for any follower of the traditional way must accept the possibility that the opponent's occasional blow at least, is going to strike home. Yet how many martial artists fold up, even with a relatively light blow to the solar plexus? Such weakness could prove lethal in a true fighting situation so it is vital to strengthen your muscles until you can take quite hard blows to the body.

We have already considered the fourth point in Chapter 7 which deals with body weapons. This concerns the toughening of your hands and feet so they can deliver a fearful blow without fracturing themselves in the process. If striking with power is one half of the equation, then turning your body weapons into effective bludgeons is the other half. This does not, of course, exempt you from the need for accuracy in technique application, though it surely gives you a wider margin for error.

The fifth point concerns skill. If you are weaker than the opponent, then the protection afforded by skill looms large between you and possible defeat. There is no doubt that a skilful martial artist can do much to offset a physical disadvantage by avoiding the opponent's attack while striking home with his own blows. This follows on from what we said earlier in that the student must be able to channel available energy effectively through toughened body weapons in order to stand a chance of winning.

The Chinese martial tradition is not short of philosophers, though it is the German, Klaus von Clausewitz who springs immediately to mind on the sixth point of fighting strategy. That is, the best form of defence is attack. Many Chinese traditions favour the view that when you are resolved to fight, then attack the opponent before he attacks you! There is no necessity to block the opponent's punch when you can beat him to the attack. This assumes, of course, that a fight is inevitable – that the person racing at you whilst brandishing a spear is not simply rushing to embrace you!

The seventh point is: never retire from attack, being content merely to block the opponent's hands. The student must take control of the situation by advancing into the opponent. Remaining still provides the opponent with an easy target upon which he can precisely range his technique. On the other hand, if you move into him, then he may still be able to hit you but you will have reduced the efficiency of his technique by at least a little. Of course, this does mean that you must be capable of taking a punch or two in the process!

Combat Tactics

An attack takes a finite time and distance over which to develop energy, so the earlier you interrupt it, the less effective it is. This means looking for the earliest signs of a committed attack and responding immediately. As soon as committed movement is discerned, attack swiftly and with strength. The Shaolin strategy is simple: put the opponent down as quickly as possible.

None of the Shaolin systems appear to have placed all their confidence in the delivery of a single technique. Great stress was laid upon the ability to be able to rain down a barrage of hard blows on the opponent. The opponent might be able to block the first two or three but eventually one must get through. However, for multiple attacks to be effective, the blows must come one after the other, without a pause between them – a pause in which the opponent might be able to recompose himself. Furthermore, they must come from different angles and aim at different targets. Only by this means is the opponent's defensive system overloaded. The object is to maintain pressure, even if one of the opponent's counters gets through and strikes you. At some stage, the student will close with the opponent and, when that happens, the short-hand boxer comes into his own. The average opponent will only be able to use his knees, elbows, or head. The knees are not recommended because lifting a foot off the ground with the opponent so close is not sensible and, in any case, a knee attack is only effective against an untrained or weaker opponent. On the other hand, an elbow attack is very dangerous, as can be a head butt.

A larger opponent is not necessarily stronger or more resolved, but if you don't attack him powerfully from the outset, then his sheer size may come to frighten you. He may have the greater strength, so use your skill. A sound fighting strategy does not pit inferior against superior strength but off-sets the opponent's advantage by a greater application of skill. Chinese martial legends abound with illustrative stories about a stork defeating a bear, through the former's use of distance, timing and accuracy. One can at least see what they are getting at, even if the stories themselves are a little hard to swallow.

Ultimately, of course, it does not matter which martial arts system you study – whether internal or external, long-hand or short-hand. The final decider is the martial artist himself. Think of the system as the hardware and the person who operates it as the software. Neither can function without the other, and so it is with the martial arts. The final point must therefore be to avoid both anxiety and over-confidence. The supreme martial artist trains until he can slip easily into a state of relaxed mindfulness in which the body does not impose its will on the mind, or vice versa. It appears that the combination of Ch'an philosophy and Shaolin martial art practice was able to achieve this.

10 The Shaolin Pole

It is said that Shaolin is the home of pole techniques, so a study of pole usage is relevant to this study of Shaolin Temple Boxing. It may be that there is a useful spin-off from this study because, although the carrying of quarterstaffs may not be appropriate in this day and age, training in the club with such a weapon can benefit both accuracy and power delivery. The movements of the pole simulate unarmed striking techniques so there is a good transference of learning between the two disciplines. Moreover, the weight of the pole and its momentum strengthen the arms, shoulders and chest muscles, so allowing the student to develop more powerful punches.

People who, as a result of their training or occupation, were already strong found the pole an effective weapon. Thus farmers and fishermen are generally associated with effectiveness in pole training. However, this effectiveness was not a question of sophistication or nicety, it was simply a case of raw power.

The pole was also a weapon of choice for Buddhist monks – particularly those who wandered the countryside. It proved a help when walking over difficult terrain and it is a useful weapon which, in the hands of an expert, is effective even against sword-wielding warriors. If a Buddhist is to use a weapon, then perhaps a pole is the least of available evils because it can be used without necessarily spilling the opponent's blood. The old adage of never drawing a weapon unless you intend to use it is apropos here. Unsheathe a sword and you are virtually committed to shedding blood. The staff, on the other hand, need administer no more than a bruise, though it is easily capable of shattering a sword blade.

The staff is thus a good police weapon and that is why it survives today in the police forces of the world. Its one disadvange is its size. This precludes its efficient use in confined spaces. The short stick has an advantage here, though the latter requires very supple wrists and powerful forearms to deploy with sufficient speed.

Above: The stick is also an effective weapon – provided you have supple wrists and strong forearms

Left: Training with the pole increases upper body strength and endurance

Nowadays, Shaolin pole training is not used to teach students how to fight. It is simply a relic of traditional martial art practice that persists to the present day. Nevertheless it is a relevant part of modern training because it is a means of training yourself, through the application of an internal, rigorous discipline. Many modern schools don't have their own pole training systems and share the 'six-and-a-half-point pole techniques' with other styles. These they modify according to their own requirements.

Good schools teach the students to regard the pole as an extension of their own bodies, just as fists and feet are. The student is the major element in pole training because the pole has no power of itself. The badly taught student misunderstands this and so comes to rely totally upon his weapon.

Principles and Techniques

Traditional pole training comprises two main elements. The first is the development and application of internal practice. The second is the development and application of skill. The skilled user must be able to put something of himself into the movements of the pole, using it with a tranquil mind that is uninhibited by fear or anxiety. The monks of Shaolin seemed to be able to do this and tales abound of their calm courage. They appeared to have no fear in the face of swords and spears, but neither did they show any evidence of that reckless courage which throws away life and is futile. Unfettered by fear or anger, they were able to use their poles with such consummate skill that even the Japanese pirates who vanquished them were moved to admiration by their skill and lack of fear.

The user puts energy into the pole through the application of mental resolve and physical effort. Both aspects are important and if either is deficient, then the pole moves in a weak manner. It may be possible to strike someone quite hard, yet not hard enough to inflict serious injury.

The pole must always be under tight control and the path through which it travels is always direct. The inexperienced student is unable to control the energy which he puts in with the result that the pole cuts curved paths through the air. Furthermore, the novice's level of accuracy may be unacceptably low, so even if the pole is used with sufficient power, it nevertheless misses the intended target. Sometimes the target is quite small. You may, for example, want to strike the opponent's foot in order to dissuade him from coming after you. The best way to train for this is to aim the tip of the pole at a particular target on the floor and be able to strike it hard from different angles.

Nowadays the emphasis in pole training seems to be on acquiring technical excellence. This is a hollow target to aim for because, ultimately, the student is defeated by advancing age. The technically gifted performer possesses this excellence only while he is young and fit but when he gets older, nothing is left. Concurrent mental training develops awareness and skill to a great degree, and that development is not sapped by age. It may be that the older martial artist can no longer move the pole with the same

138

Long training poles are held close to one end. Different schools use different grips

speed and explosive power which he utilised as a young student, but no matter! In their place has developed an economy of effective movement which uses only as much effort as is necessary to defeat the opponent.

The Shaolin pole is reckoned to be approximately two metres in length, though longer versions are known. The latter, though, are unwieldy and served as training aids for the shorter pole. In all cases the pole is made from a hard, dense wood that is smoothed to a fine finish. The decorations that one sometimes sees on modern poles had no place on the original weapons.

The pole is quite heavy and a minimum level of strength is necessary to deploy it properly. Without this degree of strength, you might as well not pick up the pole at all! Choose a shorter or lighter pole and learn techniques with that. Working with a lighter pole will eventually help you to move up to the full-size pole. Some

Lift the pole in front of your shoulders, making sure it is perfectly horizontal

Shaolin monks trained with an iron-sheathed pole that was used to great effect against cavalry. This, of course, requires great strength in the arms and upper body without which the iron pole is difficult to retrieve quickly enough to cover any openings caused by the first swing.

The pole can be swung into the target, in which case maximum force is developed in the distal third of its length. I have seen a swinging pole shatter a hard wooden chair, so there is no doubt that it could inflict serious damage on a human target. Large swings are effective at clearing a swathe through ranks of adversaries though it is not always advisable to use them against single opponents. They have only to dance back out of range, then swoop in as the heavy pole is being retrieved. Longer training poles are sometimes up to four metres in length! These are

140

Then thrust the pole out from your body

extremely heavy and, once moving, they possess great momentum. To make matters worse, they are gripped close to one end, with the hands no more than a shoulder-width apart.

Begin by practising how to hold and wield the pole which is the right size for you. Some schools grip with the right hand palm-upwards and the left palm-downwards. Other schools hold the pole with both hands in a palm-upwards grasp. The feet are open by about a shoulder-width. The pole is first drawn up in front of the shoulders, then it is thrust out from the body. The pole must be horizontal as this is done. Thrust the pole downwards in front of the hips and repeat the whole sequence a number of times. Practise in front of a mirror to check that the pole is horizontal and aim for short, explosive movements of the arms.

Begin the same sequence of moves but this time, as the pole

141

Thrust the pole to the side, straightening your right arm fully

reaches shoulder height, thrust it out strongly to the side in an attacking strike, twisting your grip as you do so. Your right arm straightens fully and the pole moves in a horizontal unwavering line. Then draw the pole quickly back and bend your knees whilst keeping your back straight. Bring the right hand back to your knee and lift the tip of the pole. Straighten up and raise both arms in a deflecting block, so the tip of the pole now points downwards. Then turn your hips and strike downwards onto the mat. Drop down to your knees and raise the tip of the pole once more, then thrust it out from the body and into the opponent's face. Repeat the full sequence of movements, each time trying to increase the amount of power transmitted.

There is no need to slavishly follow the above sequence, and students are at liberty to vary their body angle and targets as they

Top: Press down with your rear hand, so the tip of the pole flicks upwards
Above: Turn your hips away and raise the pole above your head

143

Above: Thrust the pole into the imaginary opponent's face

Opposite above: The main object is to be able to move quickly and to strike with accuracy

Opposite below: You must be able to strike a small point with great accuracy and power – it is no use missing the opponent's foot!

wish. The main objective is to be able to move quickly and strike with power and accuracy. Remember, the pole moves in straight lines. Check all aspects of your performance by training in front of a mirror. A technique may feel correct yet when you see it reflected you will be able to see mistakes. By correcting these, you develop a feel for the correct technique and through constant repetition this feel is grooved into the brain so that eventually you can perform all

144

Knock the descending strike to the side with your block

the movements accurately, without needing to check against your mirror image. Lack of feedback at the all-important early stage means that you may acquire the feel of a wrong technique and, thereafter, it will be more difficult to correct.

The two-metre pole is the classic Shaolin weapon though many variations in length and thickness were used by the monks. Both ends of the shorter pole are used and a great amount of upper-body flexibility is required. The pole is gripped equidistantly on either side of the centre, though again, individual preferences have been noticed when studying the old prints. The most important thing is that the hands are mobile and slide around the pole as it moves. This can pose a problem in that a loose grip allows the pole to be jarred from the hands. The training whereby the gripping action is

146

Horizontal strikes are countered by turning into them

localized in the lower forearm muscles is directly transferable to the Shaolin punching action. The wrists must be firm and the elbow joints resilient so they can absorb the shocks of impact.

The pole is generally gripped in a mixed underhand – overhand grasp, though this too can change to suit the circumstances. Begin training with a partner, exchanging strikes and blocks in a preagreed pattern. Move the pole in short arcs, aiming at the opponent's knees, thighs, wrists, forearms, ribs and head. Counter these cuts with short, chopping blocks that meet the opponent's pole with a considerable degree of force. Strike with the distal third of the pole into the opponent's cuts. Thrust directly into the opponent's cut – don't just interpose your pole between the opponent's and its target. Use both ends of your pole and

147

A strike delivered whilst you are moving forward is especially powerful

always try to redirect the energy of attack. Thus, a descending strike to your head is not simply blocked by laying your pole at 90 degrees to it. Rather, you strike into the descending pole, knocking it *to the side*. Remember, if you don't do this, then a really powerful attacking blow may well break your pole and carry on through to strike you.

Horizontal attacks are the most difficult to block since an unwise blocking action can skip the opponent's pole into your knuckles. The way to counter this is to turn your hips in behind the block, so the opponent's pole rebounds from yours. Then swing your own pole in an overarm strike to the opponent's head.

The importance of developing considerable power will become apparent once you have been training for a while. Allow your feet

148

Be careful when attacking with the butt of your pole

to swivel as you strike, using your hips as an additional source of power. Make your stance changes fluidly and use stepping movements to control distance and angle. An attack delivered whilst in motion has the energy of the moving body added to the momentum of the pole itself. Maximum impact is generated when your centre-line is facing the opponent and you allow a short follow-through.

Be careful when using straight thrusts with the butt ends of the pole. These are dangerous because the pole's cross section is narrow and it can find its way through the smallest openings. A sudden short step forward adds considerably to the thrust's impact and old training prints show that the opponent's stomach, face and throat were favourite targets. Use elbow action to extend the

149

length of the thrust and stiffen them by twisting the grip in opposite directions as the pole strikes home.

The Short Staff

The short staff, or stick, is another Shaolin weapon of great versatility. Experts were said to be able to weave an impenetrable wall around themselves simply by swinging the stick quickly in figure-of-eight curves. The hardwood stick is less likely to inflict serious injury though there is no doubt that it could knock the opponent unconscious or break his limbs! The stick was favoured by older monks who found the heavy pole a little too taxing for their muscles.

As you might expect, the two weapons share some similarities in usage though the stick was most often deployed against an unarmed opponent. It was swung hard into the opponent's limbs as the latter attempted to punch or kick. Inserted under the

Left: Swing the stick into the opponent's limbs

Above: Insert the stick under the opponent's arm . . .

opponent's arm, it applied considerable leverage against the shoulder joint and could be used to hold him until help arrived. A wide double-handed grip allowed the stick to be thrust against the opponent's face, or against his leg as he kicked.

152

Left: . . . and use it to apply leverage to his shoulder joint

Above: A double-handed grip is used when the stick is thrust into the opponent's face

11 Other Shaolin Weapons

The previous chapter was devoted entirely to the pole because that weapon, more than most, was to become the symbol of the Shaolin fighting monk. This chapter will consider the other weapons available.

When it comes to weapons, the Chinese must surely rank as the most gifted inventors. Who else could have invented a solid-fuel cruise missile when other races were still slinging stones at each other? As you might, then, expect, the Chinese armoury has been packed with more varieties of weapon than just about any other country you can think of. To be sure, some weapons – such as the staff – have been constant in their size, shape and usage over more than a thousand years. Others, such as the sword, have lengthened, shortened, developed double edges from a single edge, bent, straightened and changed from single-handed to double-handed designs and back again. It therefore follows, in this brief overview, that all we can hope to achieve is a very general picture of the type of weapons used by Shaolin Temple throughout its long martial history.

Spears and halberds were both used by the monks at various times. The spear is a stabbing weapon, the halberd (*quan do*) is a combination stabbing – cutting weapon. Spears were either short or long, depending upon their use. Short spears were balanced for throwing and there are some remarkable prints of early Shaolin Temple practice which show monks batting incoming spears out of the air with their arms. Longer spears were used against cavalry but their very length made them difficult to use outside of that context. Spear variants, such as the trident, were common and were used to trap and snap sword blades caught between the tines. The halberd was used in a combination manner – to hack and slash, and to thrust at the opponent. This is a much heavier weapon and the large combination head gives it considerable momentum when swung. Therefore the emphasis is on shorter

154

arcs, with a drawing movement at the end to facilitate the cutting action. Both spears and halberds are distance weapons. The skilled user could injure the swordsman while the latter was too far away to pose an immediate threat.

The sword is a shorter combination weapon, much favoured in hand-to-hand combat. Each type of sword required different practice forms. Heavier swords were used to chop at the target, their considerable weight allowing them to cleave through light-weight armour. There is an interesting correlation between the size and weight of the swords and the armour against which they were pitted. Lighter swords mean faster actions, with accuracy assuming a proportionately greater role. Straight swords are better for stabbing than curved blades but the latter are more effective at slashing.

Sometimes the sword was used together with a shield; at other times two swords were used together. Many traditional practice forms exist to the present day and illustrate how the two-sword system was used to weave a slashing wall of steel around the practitioner. When fighting a spearsman, the sword-bearing warrior would have to avoid the jabbing tip, whilst waiting for the opportunity to close inside the longer weapon's attack radius. This required considerable agility, plus a knowledge of distance and timing; concepts which were then applied with great success in the unarmed Shaolin systems.

The introduction of a well-developed new weapon to a battle-field has been known to bring striking results. Though not perhaps an appropriate example, the armoured knights of Frederick Barbarossa created havoc with their massed coordinated cavalry charges until their adversaries learned the name of the game and replied in kind. The new weapon is effective because no tactics for dealing with it have been evolved by the opposing warrior caste. Eventually, however, such tactics are developed and the advantage of the new weapon is nullified.

The Shaolin monks were particularly adept with such unusual weapons as the bladed rings, the iron pole, the three-section staff, the whip, and the chain with a weight on the end. Such weapons appeared only in small numbers, so battlefield accommodation to their use was considerably delayed.

The monks' expertise with weapons does not explain the great successes that they are credited with. We read of how 13 or 14 of them were able to put an army to flight but when the circumstances are examined, it seems more likely that the army in question was contained within a geographical bottleneck and was already under great pressure from the opposing forces. The sudden appearance of fearless fighters in the rear and on the flanks, their numbers exaggerated by the narrow confines of the battlefield, may well have gone some way towards tipping the balance. What is not likely is that such a small group was able to take on and defeat an overwhelming force in head-on conflict. Eventually, sheer weight of numbers is enough to crush any small band, no matter how skilled. It therefore follows that reports of the monks' successes failed to give an accurate account of the size of the opposing force and/or failed to give sufficient credit to the contribution of those soldiers fighting alongside the monks.

The increasing usage of firearms led to the monks withdrawing from the battlefield, though retaining their role as a militia in their own lands. Despite the fact their weapons were now obsolete they continued to train with them, though the reason for doing so now shifted. It was no longer necessary to consider each move in a life or death way. Therefore elements of ritual and flourish could be added and less interesting moves taken out. Weapons training remained one of the ways through which the Ch'an monk could practise his philosophy, though his life no longer necessarily depended upon it.

APPENDIX:

A Thumbnail Sketch of Chinese History

Since this book discusses the development of a martial art system in terms of its historical context, it is useful to consider also the wider social picture into which martial art development at Shaolin fits.

The earliest record of a civilization in the area we now call China is that surviving from prehistoric times. The largest concentration of remains of the primitive Shang people have been found in the provinces of Shensi, Shansi and Honan, though more scattered evidence is found spread over a much wider area. The Shang used primitive agriculture and bronze tools and weapons.

The Shang gradually gave way to what is called 'The Warring States' period which is reckoned to have lasted from the 11th to the 3rd century BC. During this time, the Shang were gradually replaced by the Chou. The latter peoples came to dominate most of northern and north-eastern China, controlling this vast area by conferring grants of lands to overlords. These in turn gave grants of land to their retainers, so a feudal system operated.

The first capital was near the modern city of Hsi-an though, after 771 BC, the centre moved to the vicinity of the modern city of Lo-yang. Central administration began to break down as the feudal fiefs became stronger and internecine strife broke out between them. One fief strove against the next, the more effective gradually subsuming those less able to defend themselves until by the 3rd century BC, there were a mere handful of strong fiefs, and a king who ruled in name only. At this time the north-western Ch'in fief (based in the Wei River valley) overcame its remaining rivals and, by 221 BC, it had established control as far south as Kwangtung. A centralized administration was imposed but this broke down by early 207 BC, to be replaced by the Han.

The Han Dynasty enjoyed more than four hundred years of rule, uninterrupted except for a brief interregnum from AD 9 to 25. The population steadily increased until by the time of the first

157

recorded census in AD 2, it had reached 57,671,000. The majority of these lived in the north. The Han Dynasty finally collapsed in AD 220, giving way to the turbulent Three Kingdoms period. The name relates to the three regional states which between them controlled China during that period. The western Chin State briefly took over control of China during AD 265 but soon lost it again in the turmoil that was to continue until AD 589.

We next enter a period of Chinese history that is of particular relevance to us. Southern China remained under the control of a series of comparatively stable regimes which succeeded in gradually extending Chinese influence over much of the south and south-east. The north, however, remained unstable and it was invaded several times by foreign tribes. During the 5th century, northern China was eventually reunified under the Wei Dynasty. North and south reunified under the Sui Dynasty in AD 589 but stability was shortlived. The Sui became virtually bankrupt in terms of influence and money, following a costly series of foreign wars. It fell to the succeeding T'ang Dynasty in AD 617. The T'ang Dynasty is the era of flourishing martial-art practice, when Chinese influences spread far afield into Korea, Okinawa and Japan. It now becomes clear why the name 'T'ang Hand' is so widely known in these countries. The T'ang Dynasty persisted between 618 and 907 and reached its zenith around AD 742. However, it too fell victim to the power blocs arising out of the need to establish regional administration and control. Although persisting in name until AD 907, the T'ang Dynasty effectively ceased to exert national control as of AD 881.

The T'ang Dynasty was replaced by a period known as 'The Ten Kingdoms' during which several states competed between themselves. From 907 to 960, a series of five northern dynasties claimed to be the rightful heirs to supreme control. These claims did not carry a great deal of weight and China remained divided until AD 979 when the last of them surrendered to the succeeding Sung Dynasty. The Sung arose as a purely northern dynasty in 960, but by 979 China was reunified once more. However, the Sung were unable to regain Chinese territories in Manchuria which had been invaded by the Khitans. Despite this, population growth doubled in the period 742–1080 and by the end of the 11th century, it had reached about 100,000,000. The majority of this growth was sustained in southern and central China, whilst the population actually declined in the northern areas.

As mentioned in the previous paragraph, part of northern China

158

had been invaded by the Khitans. These set up a semi-Chinese state named Liao. This was not the only such foreign-dominated state and in the north-west another by the name of Hsi-hsia had been established by the Tanguts. Liao was subsequently taken over by a Manchurian people known as the Jurchen. These changed the name of their state to Chin and in 1127, they succeeded in driving the Sung virtually out of northern China. Thus, during the period 936–1368, most of northern China was under a series of successive foreign dynasties. These coexisted with the Sung.

Chin was subsequently invaded by the Mongols in 1234. Sung fell to them in 1278 so, at this time, China became a part of the Mongol Empire. Chin suffered brutal repression at the hands of the Mongols, though by the time they had reached southern China the Mongols had tempered their hostility. South-western China, which had previously been ruled by a succession of independent kingdoms, was also assimilated by the Mongols.

The Ming Dynasty was established in 1368 and China was reunited under a Chinese dynasty once more, for the first time in four centuries. Ming China flourished and, by 1600, the population had grown rapidly to 150,000,000. China had emerged as a great sea power under the influence of the Mongols and this continued into the Ming Dynasty. For a time, Chinese ships traded with south-east Asia, Persia and India but eventually this trade was allowed to decline. The Manchus conquered the Ming Empire in 1644. These were descended from the Jurchen who had established Chin. The Manchus set up a powerful administration and succeeded in expanding Chinese borders beyond Mongolia, Manchuria and Tibet. The population increased to 315,000,000 in 1800, and to 430,000,000 by 1850. At the height of its powers in 1800, Ch'ing China faced serious internal economic problems and rebellions. From 1840 onwards, the western powers began to exert pressure on the Chinese government.

Continuing civil unrest and confrontations with Japan and the western powers led to further concessions being granted. Japan invaded Manchuria during 1894–5 and eventually established a puppet state there which it called Manchukuo. Mongolia became an independent state and Chinese influence in Tibet lapsed. The Ch'ing Empire finally collapsed and, for a period, overall control was lost. The Chinese Communist Party controlled large areas of Kiangsi in the early 1930's until they were driven out by the Nationalists. They set up a new base at Yen-an in Shensi, from which they operated a guerilla war against the Japanese. Russian occupation of Manchuria and Inner Mongolia ensured Communist domination of these areas after the war. The civil war in 1946 resulted in the Nationalists being driven from China to Taiwan and, in 1949, the People's Republic was established with its capital in Peking.

Words and Expressions Commonly Used in the Practice of Martial Arts

Acupuncture   A form of Chinese medicine that aims to restore the body's energy balance and hence health by stimulating meridians along which vital energy flows.

Advanced student   A sophisticated stage of practice attained by a student after a long period of assiduous study.

Ankle throw   A form of trip used in some Shaolin systems.

Arm lock   A grappling technique which applies leverage across the elbow or shoulder joint, to immobilize it.

Art   A specific skill or application of skill.

Attention stance   A ritual posture of polite attention adopted by students when the teacher is explaining an aspect of training.

Augment   To strengthen a blow, strike, kick or *block* by using other parts of the body in concert with the relevant limb action.

Axe kick   A descending straight-leg kick which drops the heel of the foot onto the opponent's head or collarbones. It is rare in *Shaolin* systems, though one or two of the northern schools have been known to teach it.

Back kick   A low kick used in many *Shaolin* systems, in which the heel of the foot travels backwards into the opponent's groin, knee, or instep.

Back stance   A *stance* in which body weight is mainly carried by the rear leg.

161

Backfist A punch which uses the upper surface, rather than the front of the knuckles. Backfist is used to attack the side of head or bridge of nose.

Bak Sing Choy Li Fut A synthesis of two styles of *Kung Fu: Choy Li Fut* and northern *Shaolin*. The result is a *long-hand boxing* style which favours turning punches.

Ball of foot That area of the foot exposed when the toes are pulled back. This is sometimes used in the northern *Shaolin* schools but the heel is more heavily favoured.

Ban Ma Bu A mixed *stance*, half-way between *horse stance* and *back stance*. Sixty per cent of body weight is taken on the rear foot.

Basics The fundamental building blocks of martial art technique from which combinations are developed.

Bear One of the *five animals* used by *Hua To* in his system of exercises.

Bear claw A form of *claw hand*. Sometimes known as 'tiger claw'.

Belt A coloured sash worn to denote the stage of training attained by a student. Coloured belts are not found in traditional *Shaolin* training though they have become popular in present-day systems.

Bird One of the *five animals* used in *Hua To*'s system of traditional exercises.

Black belt The black belt signifies an advanced stage of practice, though it is not used in traditional *Shaolin* training.

Block Using a limb to deflect the opponent's punch, kick, or strike from reaching its target.

Bodhidharma The first Chinese patriarch of *Ch'an* Buddhism. He is believed to have visited *Shaolin* and resided either in or near the temple for a period of more than nine years.

Bok Mei Pai 'White Eyebrows', a style of southern *Shaolin Kung Fu* named after the nickname of its founder, a Buddhist monk. Also know as *Pak Mei* or *Pat Mei Pai*.

Bot Jum Do The short heavy butterfly knives used in pairs by practitioners of *Wing Chun Kuen*.

Boxing, Chinese   A term used to refer to the practice of Chinese martial art. See also *Kuoshu, kung fu* and *Wu Shu*.

Breaking   The practice of breaking boards and stones with the hands and feet to demonstrate the power generated in martial art techniques.

Broadsword   A large, curved, heavy, single-edged sword used in the *Shaolin* systems.

Buddhism   A religio-philosophy founded in India by Gautama Buddha. Its influence spread into China and the sect known as *Ch'an* became particularly well accepted. *Ch'an* Buddhism is closely associated with the practice of martial art.

Butterfly hand   A double *palm-heel* strike.

Butterfly kick   A double kick in which the inside edges of the feet are swung around and into the target. The second of the two kicks is usually slapped against the performer's own hand.

Butterfly Knife   A short, heavy bladed knife, used in pairs by exponents of *Wing Chun Kuen*. See also *Bot Jum Do*.

Centre of gravity   That point in the human body around which weight is evenly balanced. In the average person, that point lies inside the abdomen at the height of the navel.

Centre-line   An imaginary line passing down the front of the body and projected forward. Many schools of classical *Shaolin* training restrict each body weapon to its own side of the centre-line.

Ch'a Chuan   A northern system of *Kung Fu* developed in the 16th century and featuring large, explosive movements.

Chain   One of the unusual weapons used at *Shaolin*. The chain was made from lightweight links, it was around four metres in length and had a half-kilo weight attached to one end.

Ch'an   See *Zen*.

Chang Chuan   A northern system of *Kung Fu* that is now widely practised in Mainland China. It is a *long-hand boxing* system.

Chi   The vital energy that is produced by living things.

Chi Sau   The 'sticking hands' exercise of *Wing Chun Kuen* where opponents test each other's guard through following each other's arm actions.

Chinese boxing A term used to refer to the practice of Chinese martial art. See also *Kuoshu, Kung fu* and *Wu Shu*.

Ching Lo The twelve meridians of the body along which vital energy flows. These are used in the healing art of *acupuncture*.

Chin'na One of the first systematized grappling systems which relied upon *locks* and holds rather than on striking techniques.

Cho Chiao A northern system of *Kung Fu* noted for its high kicks.

Chow Gar A mixture of two forms of *Kung Fu*: Hung Kuen and Choy Gar. Chow Gar is a southern 'family' system.

Choy The name of the *Shaolin* monk who developed one of the five basic styles of Shaolin *Kung Fu*. The style *Choy Li Fut* is named after him.

Choy Li Fut One of the most popular of the southern Shaolin systems. It is a *long-hand boxing* system, relying upon swinging punches.

Chuan 'Fist', or 'Boxing': a general term applied to any school of Chinese boxing. Also known as *Kuen*.

Chuan'fa 'Fist-way': a general term used as above. See also *Chuan'shu*.

Chuan'shu 'Fist-art': a general term used to describe Chinese boxing in general. See also *Chuan'fa*.

Circular block A blocking technique which uses a circular application to deflect the opponent's attacking technique.

Claw hand A low-velocity body weapon in which the fingers and thumb are hooked forward. Claw hand is used to attack the opponent's face. Alternatively, it is used to take a powerful hold of the opponent.

Combination A series of basic techniques performed consecutively and/or concurrently.

Control Exercising a limitation over the amount of force employed in the execution of a technique.

Coordination The linking together of body movements with such elements as timing and distance so as to produce an effective technique.

Counterattack An aggressive response to the opponent's attack.

Crane One of the animals used as a model for *Kung Fu* techniques. There are four types of crane: blue, white, yellow and black. See also *Pak Hoke*, or *Peh Hoke*.

Crane's beak A low velocity hand weapon used in White Crane *Kung Fu*. The thumb and fingers are brought together and the strike is made with their tips.

Crane stance A *stance* supposed to symbolize the crane standing on one leg.

Crane Style Two styles of Chinese *Kung Fu*. One was developed in Tibet, the other in Fukien province.

Crescent kick A straight-legged circular kick that swings the inside edge of the foot into the target.

Da Jong A forearm-toughening exercise in which the arms are repeatedly struck against wooden spars. A traditional liniment is applied afterwards to complete the training.

Dan Tien See *Tan Tien*.

Deer One of *Hua To's five animals* on which he based his exercise system.

Deflect To change the course of an attacking technique.

Dim Mok The Chinese art of attacking the *vital points* of the body so as to produce incapacity or even death. The effects of a strike can be either instantaneous, or delayed.

Double block The practice of using two *blocks* together to sweep a large area clear of attacking techniques.

Double Sword A linked sword that can be separated into its two components which may then be used independently.

Dragon's head fist A *one-knuckle fist* in which the middle joint of the middle finger is thrust forward and used as the striking area.

Drunken style A series of movements found in a number of *Kung Fu* styles which simulate the weaving and unsteady actions of a drunk.

Eagle claw style   A school of *Kung Fu* in which *claw-hand* strikes are favoured. The style also uses high kicks and jumping techniques.

Edge of foot   Inner edge of foot is that on the big toe side; outer edge is on the little toe side.

Edge of hand   *Knife hand* is the little finger edge of the extended hand. *Ridge hand* uses the thumb-side.

Elbow   A close range weapon used in many different styles of *Shaolin* boxing.

Er Liang Men   'Two Elements Boxing': a style of *Kung Fu* based upon notions of duality in nature, e.g., *Yin and Yang*.

External system   Any system of *Kung Fu* that generates its power through obvious muscle action. See *Wai Chia*.

Feng Chi Shu   An alternative name for *Chin'na*.

Fist   The closed hand used in striking techniques. Various parts of the fist are used as weapons.

Five animals   The *tiger, bird, deer, monkey and bear*: the five animals used in *Hua To*'s system of traditional exercises.

Focus   The method of concentrating the energy of a particular technique on a specific target.

Follow-through   The continued movement of a technique after it has passed the point of *focus*.

Follow-up   A technique which logically follows another.

Foot sword   A name occasionally used to describe the outer edge of the foot.

Forearm   That part of the arm, between wrist and elbow, that is used in blocking techniques.

Forearm block   A blocking technique using the *forearm*.

Form   A series of basic techniques performed in order (see also *pattern*). Also used to describe the appearance of a technique, i.e., 'good/bad form'.

Forward stance   A *stance* in which body weight is projected forwards. It is sometimes used when advancing into a punch.

Fou Tou Ou   The hook and crescent sword used in some styles of *Kung Fu*.

Free-style sparring   Unprogrammed *sparring* between two practitioners.

Front kick   A kick delivered with the heel. The hips face in the direction of the kicking action.

Front-leg kick   A kick delivered with the front foot. Such kicks are weaker than their rear-leg counterparts and are used simply as checking techniques.

Fu   The battleaxe.

Fu Jow Pai   A *Shaolin* system based upon the movements of the tiger.

Fut Gar   A style of *Kung Fu* using both soft and hard techniques. There are northern and southern variants, both of which favour hand techniques above kicks.

Grading   A modern way of assessing whether a student has advanced in skill and ability. It is associated with the giving of coloured *belts*.

Grappling techniques   Those techniques which involve closing with and seizing the opponent who may then be held, immobilized, or thrown.

Great Ultimate Fist   See *Tai Chi Chuan*.

Guard   The relation of the hand positions to the *stance*. Along with stance, this is one of the means by which a traditional master is able to judge the skill of a student.

Gung Fu   See *Kung Fu* and *Kuoshu*.

Halberd   A combination piercing and cutting spear-like weapon. *Quan Do* in Chinese.

Hammerfist   The little finger edge of the rolled fist used for *blocks* and strikes.

Hand-conditioning   Methods of toughening the hands so they become effective weapons. These involve both strengthening the bones and thickening the skin.

Hao Chuan   White Crane *Kung Fu*.

Heel Kick A thrusting or stamping kick which strikes with the heel of the foot.

Hook Sword A traditional double-edged Chinese sword with a hook to one side of the piercing tip.

Hooking forearm block A forearm *block* that uses the hooked wrist to deflect and trap the opponent's guard.

Hop Gar A style of *Kung Fu* raised to prominence by the Manchu emperors, who had their imperial guard trained in it. It consists of twelve *long-hand* and twelve *short-hand boxing* techniques.

Horse stance A wide straddle *stance* with the weight distributed equally between the two feet.

Hsing Ye An internal form of *Kung Fu* that in many ways is intermediate between the *external systems* and the more advanced *internal systems*.

Hua To The 3rd century AD Chinese physician who invented a series of health-giving exercises based upon the movements of *five animals*.

Hung Gar A major southern *Shaolin* style which uses *horse stances* and long punches.

Hung Sing The founder of *Choy Li Fut* style of *Kung Fu*.

I Chin Ching 'Muscle Change Classic', a system of exercises said to have been written by *Bodhidharma*.

I Ching 'Book of Changes': an ancient Chinese book of divination.

Internal system Any form of *Kung Fu* that generates its power from means other than obvious muscle action.

Jou Fa An ancient form of close-quarter combat using grappling techniques.

Kan Shu A form of training in which the hands are repeatedly thrust into flour, beans, rice, sand, pebbles and finally heated iron balls.

Kang Fa An old and relatively unsophisticated form of Chinese boxing characterised by straight punches and kicks.

Kay Men Bo An ingenious system of foot work used in *Hop Gar* kung fu. It has been developed from use of the *Mui Fa Jeong*, or tree stumps driven into the ground at different heights.

Knee Close-range body weapon used in many styles of *Shaolin Kung Fu.*

Knife hand Open-hand technique striking with the pad of flesh clothing the little finger-edge of the palm.

Kuen See *Chuan.*

Kung Fu The most commonly used name for Chinese martial art. The name itself simply means 'good achievement/effort'. Also known as *Gung Fu* and *Kuoshu.*

Kung-an A mystical riddle used to train the mind towards enlightenment.

Kuoshu A more correct term with which to describe the martial arts of China. See also *Wu Shu.*

Kwoon The training hall in which Chinese martial arts are practised.

Law Horn Kuen A style of *Kung Fu* characterised by intricate footwork, high kicks and jumping techniques.

Li Gar A southern style of *Shaolin Kung Fu.*

Liu Gar A southern style of *Shaolin Kung Fu* using *short-hand boxing* methods.

Lock A grappling technique using leverage to immobilize a joint.

Long-hand boxing Any system of *Kung Fu* which uses punches delivered with full movement of the elbow – from fully flexed to fully extended.

Ma Chinese name for the *horse stance.*

Martial Military, or pertaining to war.

Master A title of respect conferred upon a recognised teacher.

Mi Tsung I A highly sophisticated form of *Kung Fu* whose principal exponent was Huo Yan Chia, founder of the highly influential Ching Woo Athletic Association of Shanghai.

Mok Gar   A southern *Shaolin* school of *Kung Fu*.

Mon Fat Jong   The 'wooden man', a traditional *Shaolin* training and arm-toughening device.

Monkey   One of the *five animals* which formed the basis of *Hua To*'s system of exercises.

Monkey style   The umbrella name for a group of highly agile *Kung Fu* styles which seek to simulate the behaviour of the ape.

Mui Fa Jeong   Tree stumps driven into the ground so they stand at different heights. Used to practise footwork on in the *Hop Gar* and White Crane schools.

Nei Chia   The internal schools of *Kung Fu*. See also *internal system*.

Northern styles   An umbrella term used to describe styles of *Kung Fu* which are known to have arisen in the northern half of mainland China. They are characterized by high kicks and expansive movements.

One hundred and eight dummies   A legend based on the presence of 108 wooden men which the student was obliged to demonstrate his skill on before being allowed to leave the *Shaolin* Temple.

One-knuckle fist   A fist in which the index or middle finger is pushed out to form the striking area.

One-leg stance   A *stance* in which the exponent stands on one leg. Also called *crane stance*.

Pa Kua   'Eight Trigrams Boxing', an *internal system* of *Kung Fu* based upon circling movements and linear strikes.

Pak Hoke   A Chinese name for White Crane *Kung Fu*. Also known as *Peh Hoke*.

Pak Mei   An alternative Chinese name for 'White Eyebrow' style of kung fu. Also known as *Pat Mei Pai* or *Bok Mei Pai*.

Pak Sau   A slapping block performed with the palm of the hand.

Palm-heel   The striking part of the palm exposed when the wrist is flexed back.

Pat Mei Pai   An alternative Chinese name for *Pak Mei*.

Pattern   A series of basic techniques and combinations performed in a set order and in a set direction. See also *form*.

Peh Hoke   An alternative Chinese name for *Pak Hoke* (White Crane) *Kung Fu*.

Pole   See *staff*.

Praying Mantis   A *Shaolin* Temple style of *Kung Fu* based upon the movements of the insect of that name. The *forearms* are toughened and used to attack the opponent.

Prearranged sparring   A form of *sparring* in which the attacks and responses are agreed beforehand.

Quan Do   See *halberd*

Ridge hand   A circular strike that uses the thumbside edge of the hand.

Rising block   A forearm block that lifts diagonally up and forwards to deflect an incoming head or face attack.

Salutation   A gesture of respect in modern *Kung Fu*, usually performed by placing one closed fist against the other open palm. Protocol dictates how the two should be brought together.

San Chieh Pang   The three section *staff*.

Scooping block   A circular technique that lifts and draws the attacker's limb.

Seven stars   One of the schools of *Praying Mantis Kung Fu*.

Shaolin   The most famous of all the Chinese Buddhist temples to be associated with *Kung Fu*.

Short-hand boxing   Schools of *Kung Fu* characterised by short, jolting punches and strikes.

Shuai Chiao   An ancient grappling system similar to *Chin'na*.

Side kick   A thrusting kick striking with the heel and delivered with the body turned sideways-on to the target.

Sien Tien   An especially calm state of consciousness re-attained through meditation.

Sifu 'Teacher': a title of respect given to an advanced practitioner of *Kung Fu*.

Siu Lum The Cantonese reading of *Shaolin*.

Southern styles An umbrella name for the *Kung Fu* styles known to have originated in the southern half of China. They are characterized by short stances, low kicks and reliance upon hand techniques.

Sparring The exchange of techniques, whether programmed or unplanned, between two exponents of *Kung Fu*.

Spear hand An open-hand technique that strikes with the tips of the extended fingers. Considerable toughening is needed before this weapon can be employed properly.

Staff A wooden pole, about two metres in length, though some can be as long as four metres!

Stamping kick A downwards thrusting kick onto the opponent's knee, shin, or instep.

Stance The relation of the feet to each other.

Sticking hands See *Chi Sau*: The close-range training system used in *Wing Chun Kuen*.

Straddle stance An alternative name for *horse stance*.

Style A way of performing techniques that is clearly different from the way others practise those same moves. There are hundreds of different styles of *Kung Fu*.

Ta Cheng Chuan A style of *Internal Kung Fu* developed from *Hsing Ye*.

Ta Hsing Chuan 'Monkey boxing'; see *monkey style*.

Tai Chi Chuan '*Great Ultimate Fist*': the most sophisticated form of *Internal System Kung Fu*.

Tan Tien The main energy-producing centre of the human body. It is said to be situated near the navel. It is also known as the *Dan Tien*.

Tao A Chinese word meaning either 'The Way', or describing a single-edged broadsword.

Tiger   One of the *five animals* used in *Hua To*'s system of exercises.

Vital points   Points on the body which are susceptible to stimulation – either the health-giving stimulation of *acupuncture*, or the damaging stimulation of *Dim Mok*.

Wai Chia   The *external system* schools of *Kung Fu* which produce their effects through obvious and strong muscle action.

Wing Chun Kuen   A *short-hand boxing* form of *Kung Fu* which has become extremely popular in the last two decades.

Wu Shu   'Martial Art', the title given by China to its fighting arts.

Yang   The polarization of energy into a positive and active principle. The opposite of *Yin*.

Yin   The opposite of *Yang*, i.e., an energy polarisation that is negative and passive.

Zen   That form of Buddhism known as *Ch'an* to the Chinese.